The Presenter's E Z Graphics Kit ---

A Guide for the Artistically Challenged!

The Presenter's E Z Graphics Kit ---

A Guide for the Artistically Challenged!

Lori Backer

Michele Deck

 Mosby

St. Louis Baltimore Boston Carlsbad Chicago Naples New York Philadelphia Portland
London Madrid Mexico City Singapore Sydney Tokyo Toronto Wiesbaden

Mosby
Dedicated to Publishing Excellence

A Times Mirror
Company

Special thanks to Jackie and Jay Katz, who support and encourage us.

Publisher: Jacqueline M. Katz
Developmental Editor: Barbara Watts
Editor: Donna Sokolowski
Project Manager: Gayle Morris
Manufacturing Manager: Betty Richmond
Graphic Design: Lori Backer
Cover Design and Artwork: Lori Backer

International Standard Book Number 0-8151-1378-1

Manufactured in U.S.A

First Printing, 1996

2 3 4 5 6 7 8 9

The Presenter's E Z Graphics Kit ---

A Guide for the Artistically Challenged!

Kudos

There are some very special people in our lives who give of their ideas, creativity, spirit and loving feelings so generously. In grateful appreciation to:

Barb Watts, who is amazing and tireless!

Lynn Solem, Doug McCallum, Jeanne Silva, Bob Pike, Tim Richardson and Rich Ragan -- who give us so many ideas to shape!

Brian, Brittany, Melanie, and Melissa Deck --without whom Michele's world would be colorless!

Steven, Kelly, Aleia and Taggy Backer, who love and nurture Lori's awkward and fragile artistic soul!

And to all of you who feel artistically reluctant and challenged and yet seek to increase your ability to communicate visually, we would like to offer you special congratulations.

The Authors

Lori Backer is a talented artist, writer and presenter. She has a degree in Computer Science but threw off order and convention years ago to develop her creative side. She has extensive experience with presentations on creativity and with instructional and graphic design. Lori is the owner of The Backer Studio, Inc. and lives with her loving husband, Steven, and two big dogs, Kelly and Taggett, in Littleton, Colorado. She is also a student and teacher of Tai Chi and her continual search to sharpen her creativity and artistry shine through to all who meet her.

Michele Deck is an experienced nurse, educator, and business owner and Mom to puppies Cocoa and Mocha. She has practiced and developed her artistic abilities to the point of instructing a how- to-draw course. Michele is a high energy business trainer who owns and operates two businesses, GAMES (Gimics And Mania Educate Staff) and Tool Thyme for Trainers located in Metairie, Louisiana. Michele strives to balance over 100,000 base air miles of travel with her devotion to her husband Brian and three adorable daughters Melanie, Brittany and Melissa.

Contents

A Special Note to Begin With

Many of us are perfectly at ease speaking in front of hundreds, but feel awkward, nervous and artistically challenged when asked to draw anything more complicated than a stick person -- especially in front of others!

Yes, high technology is available and there are multiple computer graphics programs capable of creating polished visual presentations. But for many of us in the teaching, training and professional speaking professions, it is often necessary to communicate intangible ideas and concepts on the spot. We need to be able to speak in a "graphic language", creating images on papercharts, overhead transparencies and whiteboards, -- easily and spontaneously, in front of an audience!

If you have ample time to prepare for presentations, you now have everything you need to create outstanding visuals. If you have absolutely no time to prepare, we have provided ready-to-use examples that you can reproduce and use immediately.

As you begin to use the EZ Graphics Kit, look for *EZ Guide*, the artistically reluctant, challenged and witty chapter header person who will lead you through the book's sections.

EZ Guide says: "You *can* create superb visuals with little expense and without being an artist. All you need is *patience, practice and laughter!*"

The Presenter's EZ Graphics Kit is divided into four easy-to-use sections. Each section contains examples that are designed to be traced, reproduced, reduced or enlarged so that you will be able to start drawing and creating visuals right away and with relative ease.

This book is progressive and you can build skills and confidence by following the sections in order. Here is an outline of the techniques introduced in each section, along with an *EZ Guide* rating:

The Basics

EZ Guide Rating: Beginning Foundations and Warm Up

Visuals are a combination of the following key elements:

Letters	Design Space	Graphics
Colors	White Space	Borders

You will be able to create:
   Visual designs that captivate your audiences
   Easily drawn graphic pictures
   Retention building color combinations
   Unique lettering styles
   Unusual and outstanding visual borders

The Graphics

EZ Guide Rating: Beginner Intermediate

Included in this section are step-by-step panels that show you how to combine a variety of shapes and lines to create simple and easily drawn graphics. You will be able to transform ordinary circles, squares and triangles into extraordinary graphics by adding just a few extra lines here and there.

With patience and practice, you will be able to draw outstanding graphic language symbols with ease.

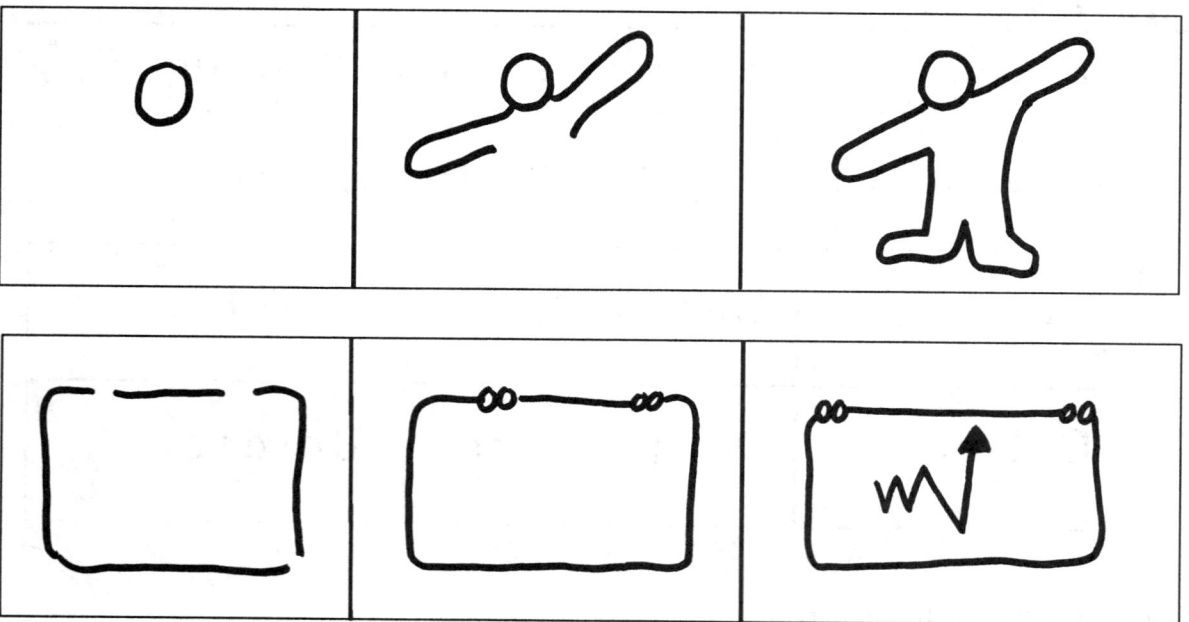

We'll also introduce you to a unique page in the book --- probably the most important page in the book, and it is so important you may wish to look at it now! We call it the *"VIG page."*

The Quick & Easy Ideas Section

EZ Guide Rating: Beginner, Intermediate & Advanced
            Requires some preparation time.

In this section you will find unusual, innovative and energy-generating suggestions for using your visual ideas and creations.

We provide you with:

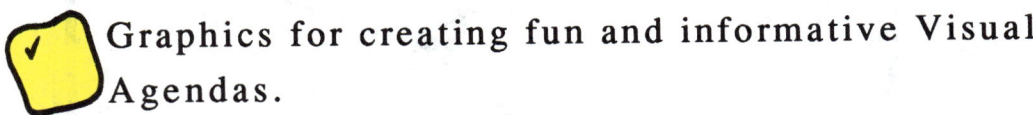 Graphics for creating fun and informative Visual Agendas.

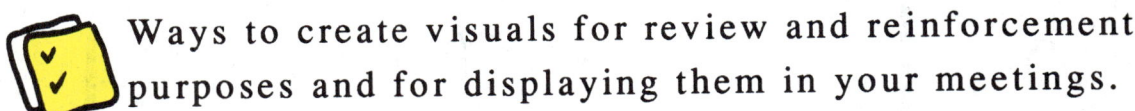 Ways to create visuals for review and reinforcement purposes and for displaying them in your meetings.

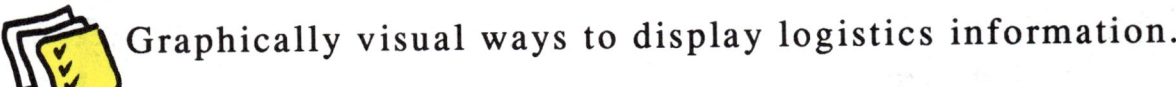 Graphically visual ways to display logistics information.

We have suggestions for preserving, recycling and displaying your visuals along with visual reproduction technique recommendations.

The Ready Mades

EZ Guide Rating: All Levels --- Minimum to medium preparation
time needed.

This section introduces you to the concept of reproducing and
enlarging pre-prepared visuals for your own use if you do not
have the preparation time to design and draw your own.

Each example is designed so that you can either freehand copy it
or trace it. You can also reproduce the example on a copy
machine and then use a Poster Printer to create poster size
visuals ready to be displayed on the wall!

The EZ Graphics Kit

EZ Guide Rating: A fabulous tool for all artistic levels!

Included in the Kit are easy to use stencils that can reduce your production time.

Stencils

Use these quick trace tools when you are creating pre-prepared flipcharts prior to your presentations.   Decide the correct placement for the graphic, trace the figure with a soft leaded pencil onto the chart paper, then fill in with colors.

Create the images on brightly colored construction paper, cut them out and attach them to your chart paper as you are presenting.

The Supply Checklist

EZ Guide Rating: For All Levels

Supplies You May Need To Get Started:

_____ Well-lit working area

_____ Comfortable, back-supporting chair

_____ Drawing paper/ sketch pad

_____ Large water based markers

_____ Small nibbed colored markers

_____ Special drawing pen (Included in Kit)

_____ Soft Lead Pencil

_____ Erasure

_____ Paper clips

_____ Scotch brand invisible/masking tape

_____ 3M Post-it Notes

_____ 3M Tape Flags

_____ Stencils (Included in Kit)

_____ Tracing paper

_____ Straight edge

_____ Access to copy machine

_____ Access to Poster Printer machine

_____ Relaxing music (Optional)

_____ Chocolate chip cookies (Optional)

_____ **The Presenter's EZ Graphics Kit!**

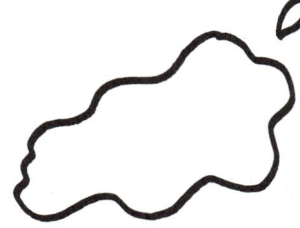

The Basics

  Borders

 **Colors**

 **Letters**

  Design

 **Images**

The Basics

Borders

EZ Guide says: "Start with simple designs for your visuals --- use a large, eye-catching title, include a graphic image related to your message, place a sub-title towards the center and frame your idea with a double line border."

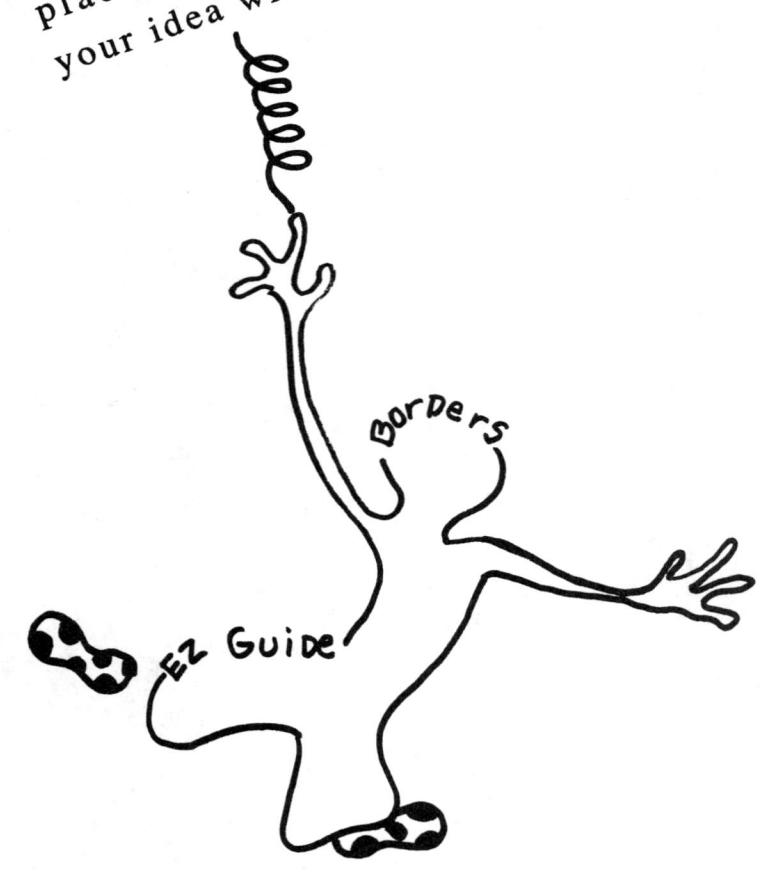

The Basics - Borders

The look of your visuals will appear more complete by placing a simple border around the content.

Borders act like frames for your ideas. A border is an easy technique that makes a big impact when used . It defines the layout space of your visual and gives it a completed, professional look.

Choose a border that encloses your information. It can be as simple as a lined box or as elaborate as your imagination can produce. Visual designers will often select a border that is related to their content, including a simple graphic or icon in the design.

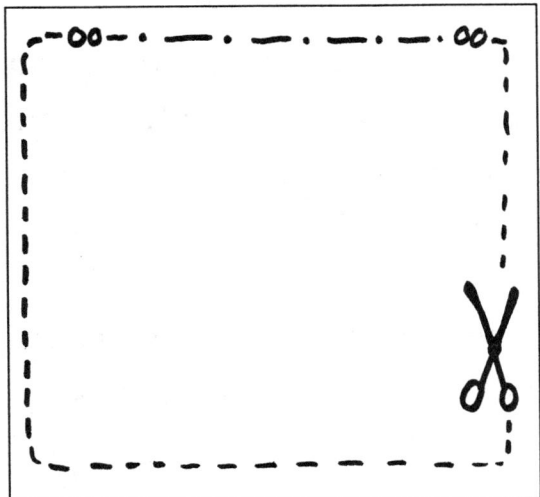

Allow your eyes to look back and forth between the two examples below. Which appeals to your eye more?

FOR TITLES

*Use capital letters
*Periodically vary size
*Use color codes to indicate importance
*Include a graphic
*Check for unity of design

FOR TITLES

graphic

*Use capital letters
*Periodically vary size
*Use color codes to indicate importance
*Include a graphic
*Check for unity of design

Your visuals will look more professional and complete if they contain a title in capital letters, usually in the upper third of the layout. The title can be in the same size print as the text, but we suggest it be in larger print.

Use bright, activating, major colors to make the title stand out. Once posted, your visual will be visually eye catching and appealing.

Use words from your subject matter in your border. Alternate thick and thin letters along with dark and light colors.

Line Borders

Vary the borders by using simple rounded lines. Add shaded areas for depth and contrast.

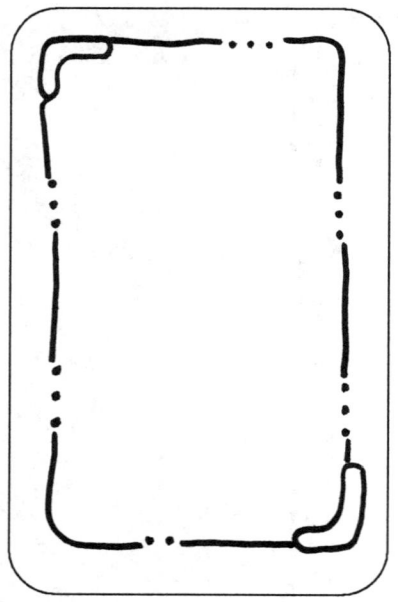
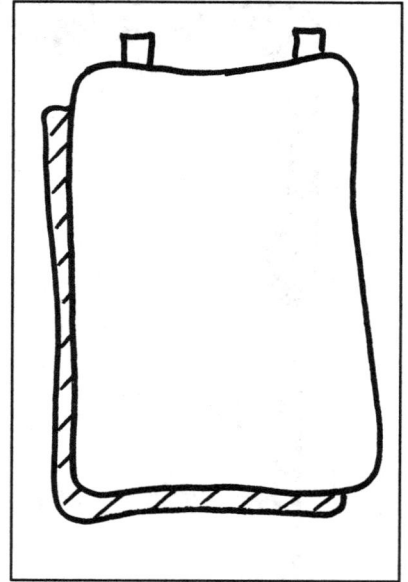

Graphic Borders

Use simple graphics and pictures for borders. Freehand the images, or use pictures and/or clipart for a different and unique effect.

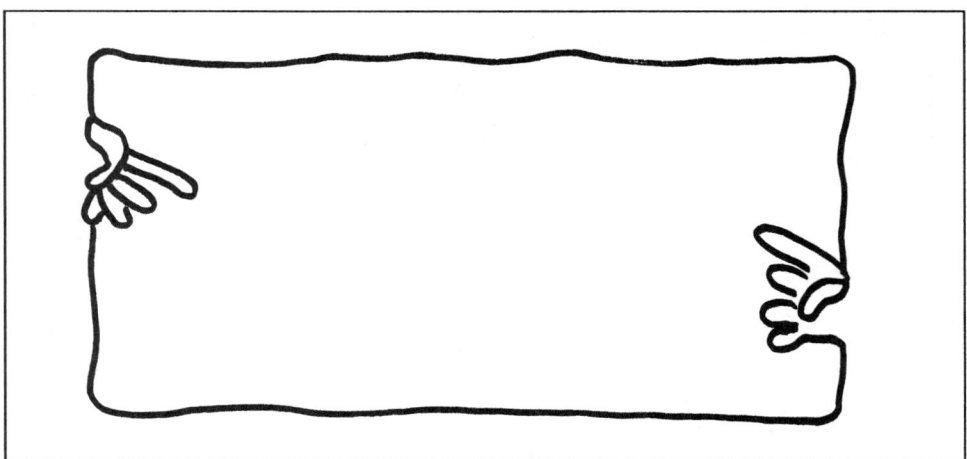

TIME TO GEAR UP . . .

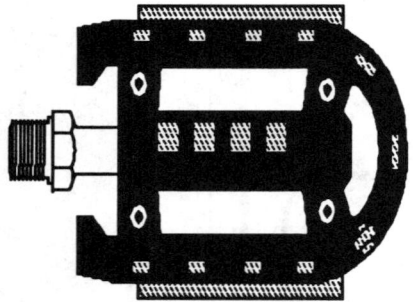

Shape Up With Safety!

Electrical Safety!

Border Samples

Border Practice Space

Border Practice Space

The Basics

Colors

EZ Guide says: "Catch your audiences attention quickly and then try to hang on to it by using three colors on your visuals."

Color can generates interest and can create excitement.
Here are some guidelines:

Guide for ACTIVATING Colors

The following colors are considered extroverted colors, intense and emotion sparking.

 **Red** is a color that evokes strong emotion. It can empower, stimulate, dramatize and symbolizes passion. It can also mean danger or disturbing information. It is good for highlighting important information, but not for content recording because, like purple, it is very dense in nature.

 **Orange** represents feelings that are friendly, cheerful, energetic, and light feeling. It is the color that represents positive thinking, and can stimulate appetite and conversation. We do not recommend it for content recording but it is good for highlighting and bordering.

 **Yellow** is the color of light and represents feelings of bright optimism. It stimulates and expands the intellect and can invite expansive thinking. It also inspires feelings of warmth and cheerfulness and can increase energy. Yellow is good for highlighting and coloring-in graphics.

Guide for PACIFYING Colors

The following colors are considered cool colors, calming and re-energizing.

 **Blue** is a blending color. This color relaxes, refreshes and cools and can produce feelings of tranquility, calmness, trust and peace. It is good for letters, borders, graphics, and backgrounds.

 **Green** is a friendly, healing color which represents growth, productivity and prosperity. This color refreshes, brings feelings of balance and encourages emotional growth. The darker shade of forest green is good for letters, borders and graphics.

 **Purple** projects boldness, power and royalty. This color comforts, assures, creates mystery and draws out intuition. It is dense in nature and should not be used as often as the colors listed above. Dense colors can quickly tire the eyes. Purple is good for bold graphics, highlighting and borders.

Guide for NEUTRALIZING Colors

The following are actually non-colors. They neither activate nor pacify and are meant to be used as frames and to show off other colors.

 **Black** represents the absence of color and can create emotions that strengthens and encourages independence. It is a good color for letters, borders and graphics.

 **Brown** is a warm earth tone color that projects feelings of strength, security and solidity. It is a stabilizing and supportive color and symbolizes the down-to-earth. It is good for letters, borders and graphics.

 **White**, like black, represents the absence of color. Use white space to lighten, expand, purify, energize, clean, unify and enliven other colors.

Guide for Highlighting Colors

Use activating colors to highlight, fill-in and shade. Avoid lettering with yellow,orange and light pink since these colors are difficult to see.

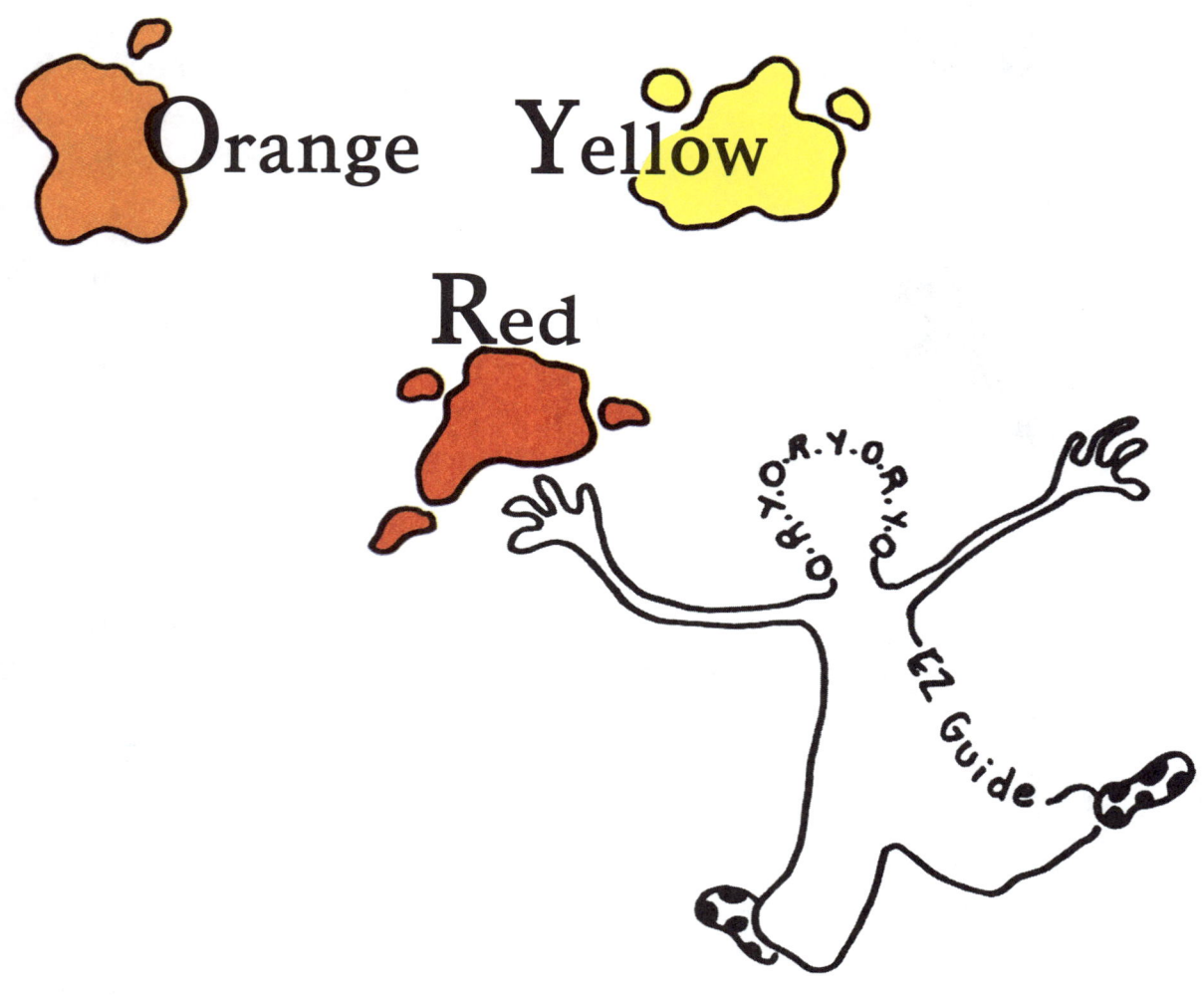

Guide for Using Major Colors

Amaximum of **three** colors can color your visuals, unless you are using a rainbow configuration of color. More than three major colors can fatigue the eye. The following are the major colors we recommend.

R_{ed}

For titles,critical words or phrases.

B_{lue}

For basic text, graphics.

G_{reen}

For non-critical words, pictures.

B_{lack}

An all-purpose color good for everything.

Rainbow Effect Example

aLues:

oNsiDer:

Color Practice Space

Color Practice Space

The Basics

Letters

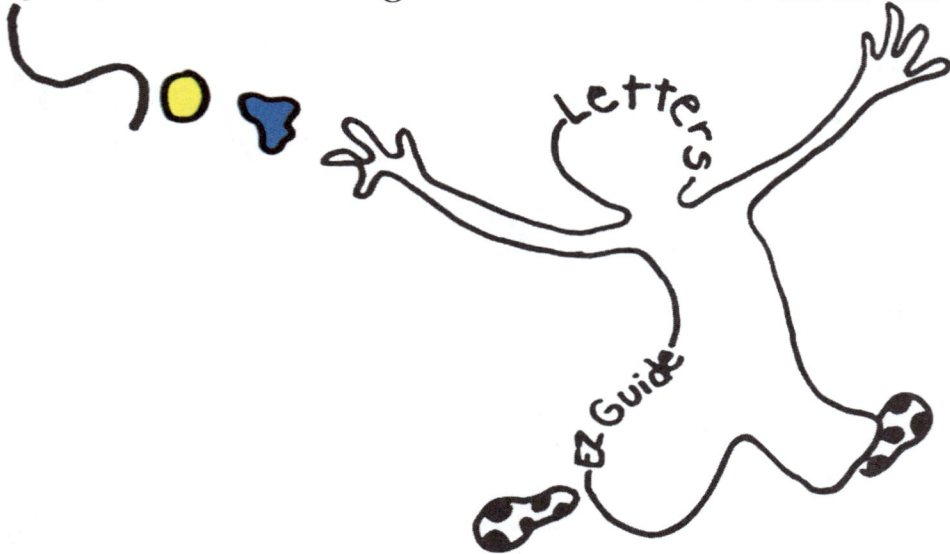

EZ Guide **says:** "To provide variety, use one or two different styles or sizes of letters. Any more than two styles, visuals can begin to look like ransom notes!

L ettering varieties can add life and sparkle to any visual. If you need letters for flipcharts, they can be generated on a computer and attached with invisible tape. There are automatic lettering machines that can provide letters as well. And there are times where you'll want to free hand letters spontaneously.

Create letters one inch in height for every ten feet from the audience. If the back of the group is twenty feet away from the visual, the letters should be two inches and so on. Use a minimum of two inch tall or larger letters on reusable flipcharts.

Choose a style of lettering that suits and compliments the message. Using very large letters conveys a loud voice, while smaller letters speak softly.

L ettering needs white space around it. This clarifies the message and helps it to stand out. Make sure that the layout of the letters is easy to read from a distance.

Letters can set the scene or create a mood by their shape or by the way they are decorated. Decorating the first letter in a word, sentence or paragraph is called illumination. Color can also add to the message and highlighting of the information. Some letters are designed to be a part of a picture, rather than being added above or below it.

The most important consideration about lettering is whether it conveys a clear message and if it is easy to read from a distance. If the message is long and complicated, use a simple style of lettering. Reserve excessively scrolled or fancy style letters for short messages or greetings as they are more difficult to read.

Provide visual contrast by coloring the background with a highlight color. Then place major color letters on top. If you use a pacifying color for the background, test that the lettering is easy to see.

When free hand drawing, to add dimension and shadows to lettering, draw the basic structure first. Then, copy the outline a bit to one side, above or below the letter. Fill in the shadow with a darker color shade than the basic letter.

Headings contain the largest letters on a visual. Use lower case letters for the text, keeping the message short and clear. Leave adequate white space around illustrations or graphics.

Highlight, underline or enlarge key points, keeping letters evenly spaced.

Align letters evenly, when free hand lettering, by using lined paper or by creating faint pencil lines called guidelines. The distance between letters should be even if you are creating uniform letters. Leave a space the size of a capital "E" between words made up of capital letters. Design a space of a small "n" between words made up of small letters.

Each letter of the English alphabet has a basic shape. Letters can be printed free-standing or joined in an overlapping style. Freestanding letters are easier to read from a distance. Create a whole new alphabet to fit any theme. Thematic alphabets can be used in many ways, relating them to a special message.

Unique lettering styles create visuals that capture the eye's attention. Freehand lettering on flipcharts is easier to do with practice. We trace the letter style we like and then using a lettering grid pad, free hand copy the traced letter, practicing several letters in a row.

It is often a good idea to warm-up and stretch the hands, fingers and wrists before drawing and lettering. The following exercises are for visual designers who will be preparing flipchart visuals freehand. If you practice the wrist and hand warmups shown below before beginning, you will find it easier to create even letters and outstanding graphics.

Wrist and Hand Warm-Up

Hold arms out in front of you.
Bend arms at the elbow, pointing hands upward.
Keeping arms, wrists and hands relaxed, begin to gently twist, turn and rotate the hands.
Increase the speed of the wrist and hand rotations until the hands are twisting rapidly.
Continue the rotations for two to three minutes.
Bring arms down and relax before beginning to draw or letter.

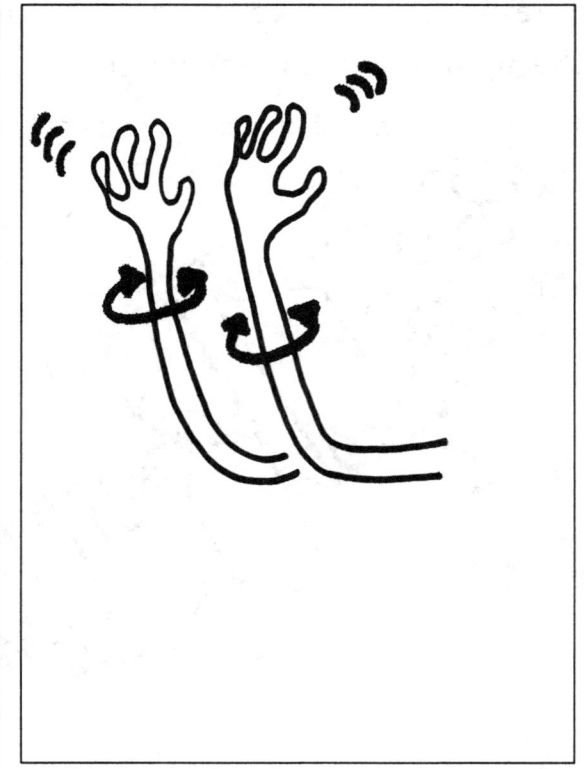

Lettering Ideas

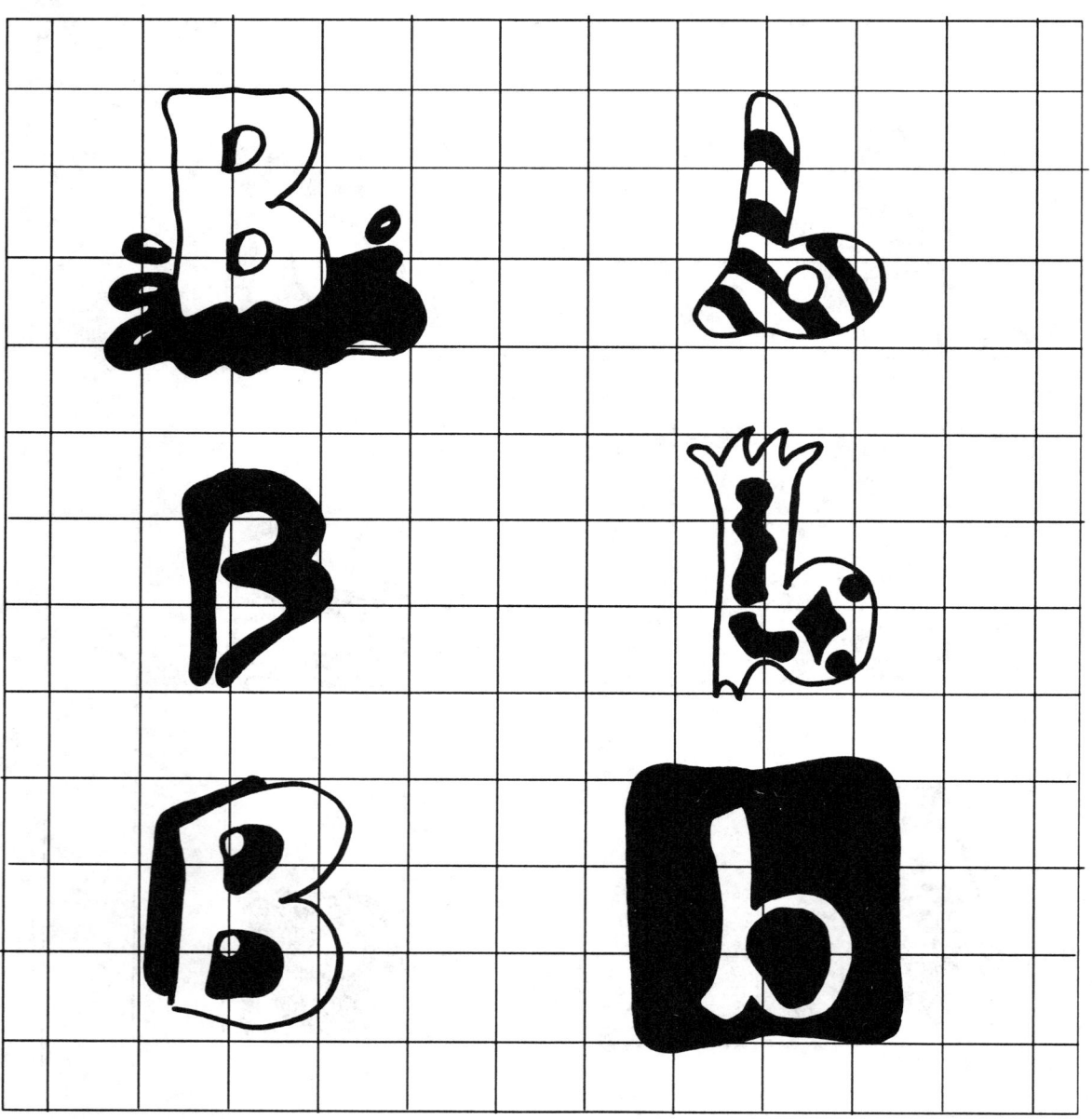

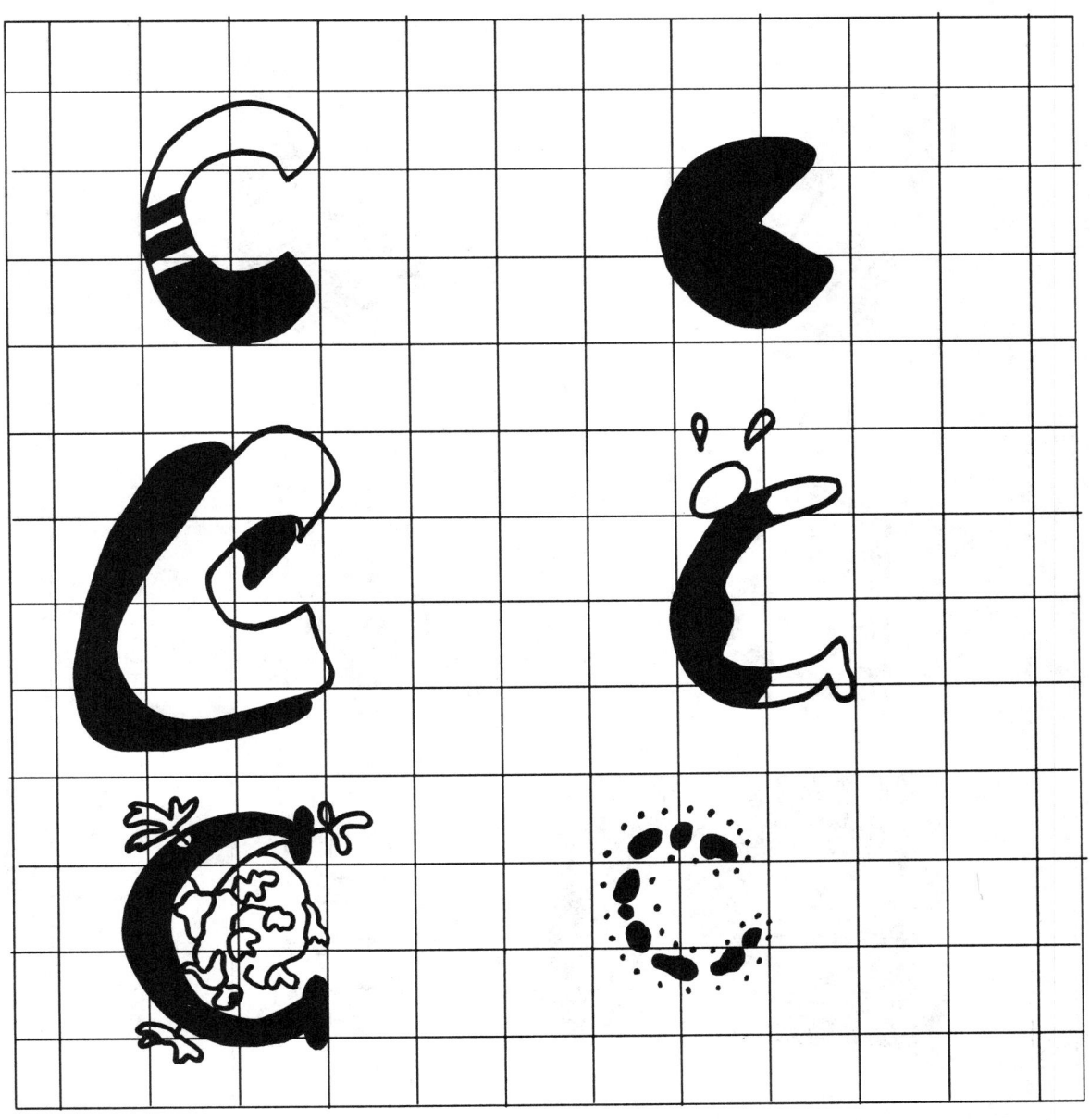

Lettering Ideas

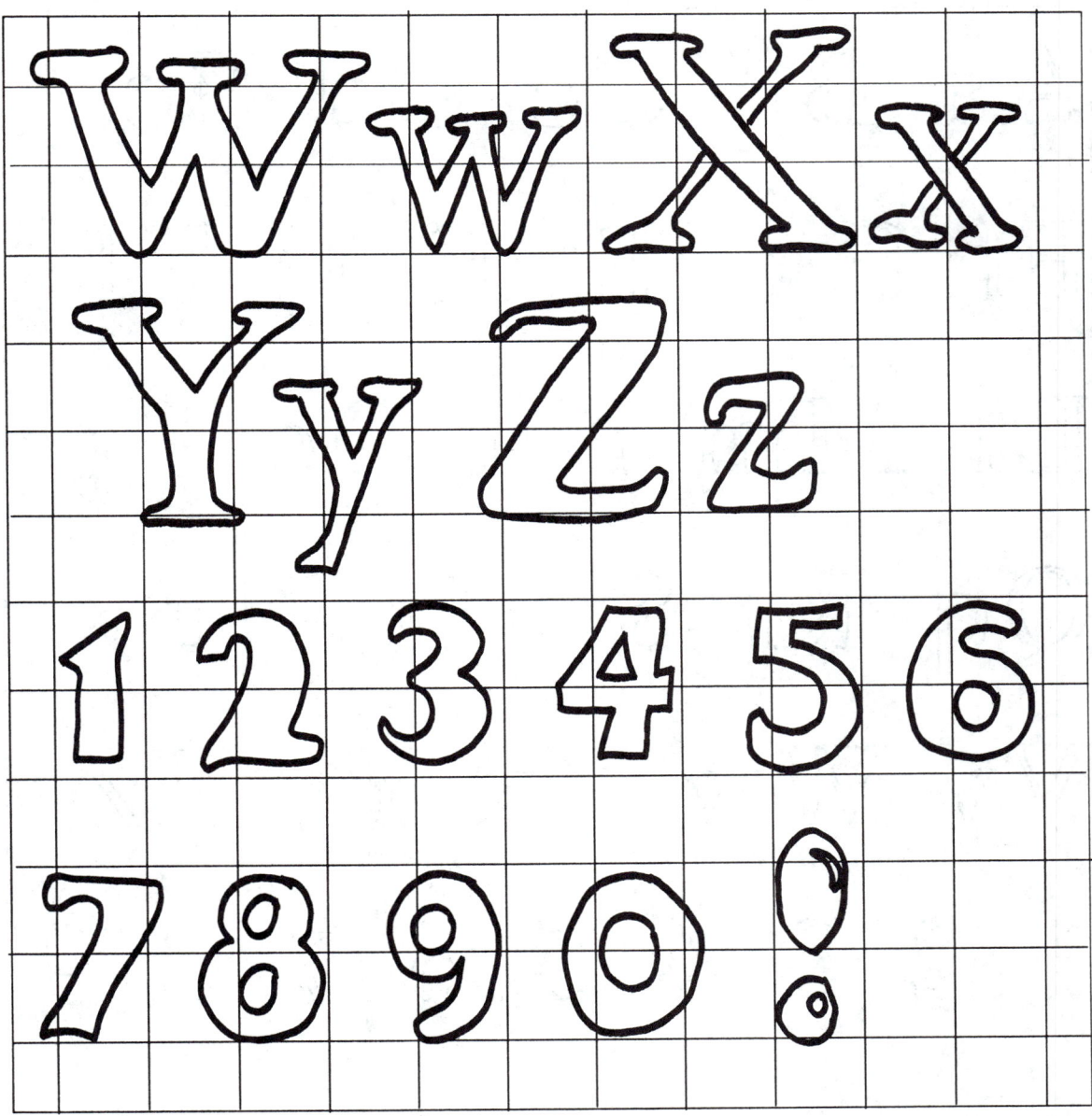

Computer Generated Alphabet

Aa Bb Cc Dd Ee

Ff Gg Hh Ii Jj Kk

Ll Mm Nn Oo Pp

Qq Rr Ss Tt Uu

Vv Ww Xx Yy Zz

1 2 3 4 5 6 7 8 9

10 (“, . ? ! : / * ”)

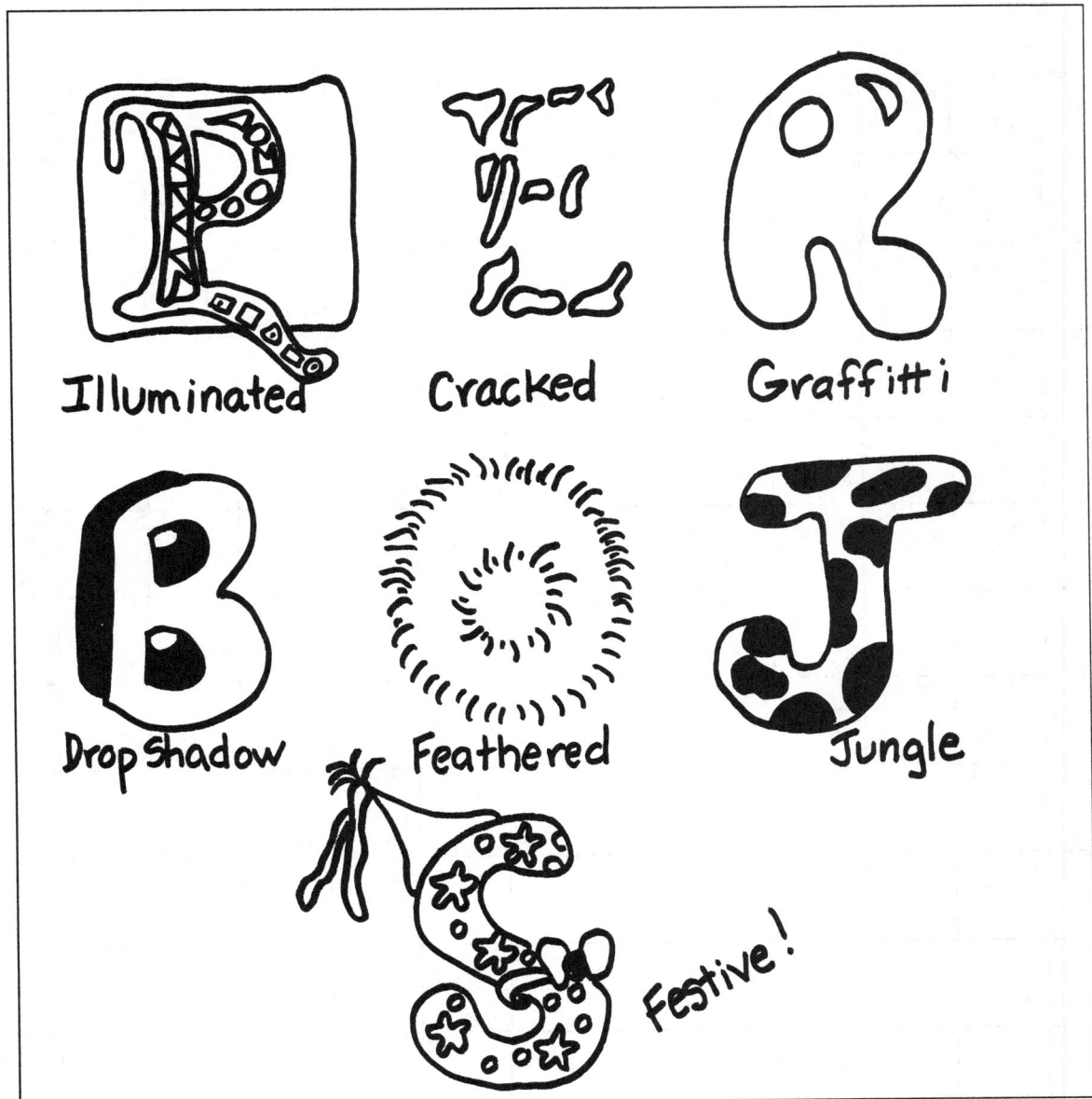

Illuminated   Cracked   Graffitti

Drop Shadow   Feathered   Jungle

Festive!

Practice Lettering Grid

Practice Lettering Grid

The Basics

Design

EZ Guide says: "Visual design can make plain, dull material interesting! Using the 6 EZ design steps along with your imagination, ingenuity and courage, your visuals will attract the reader's attention, hold it and transmit your message.

The Six EZ Design Steps

1. Layout Decision

When creating a visual, the first decision will be format selection. Choose between Portrait or Landscape.

Portrait format is the layout this book is in, the majority of the space being vertical.

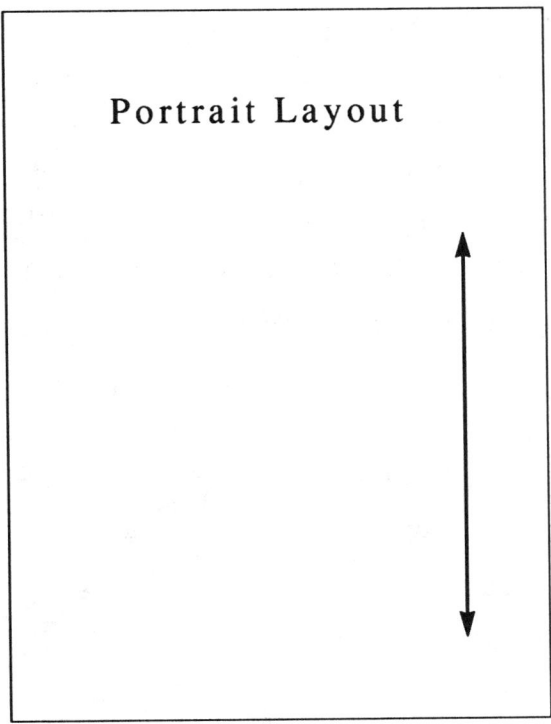

Portrait Layout

The landscape format turns the visual horizontally. This is a less frequently used format, but can be effective in regaining visual interest by changing the visual layout.

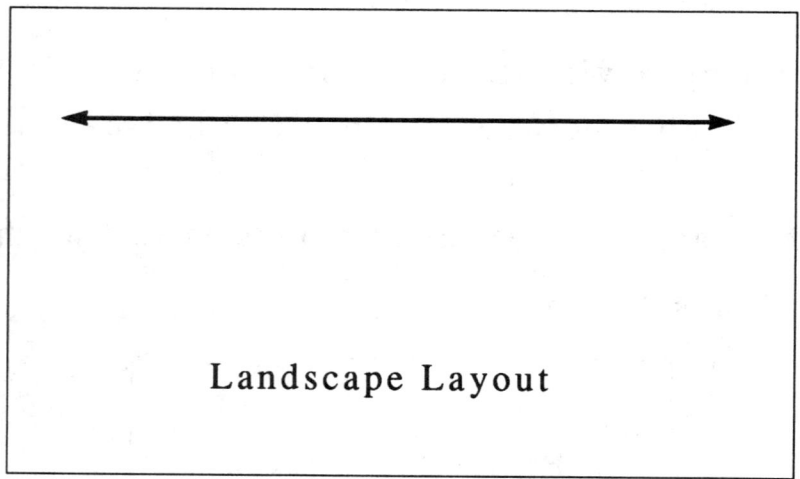

Landscape Layout

It is important to pick one format and create the majority of your visuals in that format. For visual unity in a total presentation, try to keep the design layout consistent.

Turn the paper so that one corner is up when looking to make an unusual point with flipcharts.

2. **Border Design**

The next design step is choosing the type and style of border. If a series of visuals are related, use a border to unify the message. A simple rule for borders is to keep them plain and simple so as not to distract from the main message.

3. **Major Color Decision**

Select three to four major colors for the visual. Use a combination of activating, pacifying and neutralizing colors that are easily seen. Invest in a decorator's color wheel to choose colors that compliment each other.

1. Layout

2. Border

3, Color

In the Western world, people look and read from left to right and top to bottom. Place important information at the top left of your visual and then attract the eye with lettering or graphics placed to the right. The eye's resting point will be towards the bottom left of the visual. This means once the eyes have finished reading, they will linger on the bottom left. Therefore, put something unique or interesting in this space.

4. Thumbnail Sketch

Plan the best way to position the words and pictures on your visual. Draw thumbnail sketches with pencil on paper before starting. Include a strong title that can be recognized quickly. Look at the layout and ask yourself if it is pleasing to the eye or confusing. Your goal is to transmit your message clearly.

4. Thumbnail Sketch

5. Lettering Decision

Select the size and style of lettering that will make the greatest visual impact. Main titles or headings should be larger than sub-headings. Choose lettering that catches people's attention and is easy to read at a distance remembering that the more complicated styles do not necessarily look the best.

6. Graphic/Picture Decision

Finally, create your graphic. Look at its size in relation to the overall look. Is it too big or too small? Does it need to shift left, right, up or down? Copy examples of different balance elements from graphic design magazines and books.

5. Lettering

6. Graphic

Design Example

Design Checklist

_____ 1. Layout

_____ 2. Borders

_____ 3. Colors

_____ 4. Thumbnails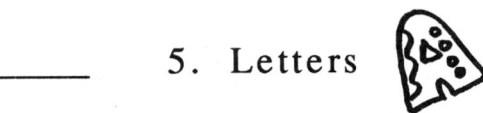

_____ 5. Letters

_____ 6. Graphics

The Basics

Images

EZ Guide says: "Make every effort to wed your graphic to your text! Graphics that are not related to the text presented can cause confusion!"

Graphic Images

Graphic images can be obtained or copied from books, clip art sources, children's coloring books or they can be drawn free-hand.

There are five different graphic image categories:

1. Photographs

The first type of image are actual photographs. Film stores can duplicate, enlarge or downsize photographs for use with your visuals. When using photographs, check for copyright protection. If they are, write for permission before using the picture.

When creating photos large enough to use on flipcharts, take a normal size picture and enlarge it on a copy machine. Attach pictures to the chart paper with double stick or invisible tape. Add color by backing the picture with a colorful piece of construction paper. You can remove and reuse the picture when the charts wear out.

If you want to reproduce a graphic onto a flipchart from a transparency, simply project the image onto the easel chart and trace the image onto the paper. Then add color, contrast and borders. Later, you can cut the picture out and reuse it on future charts.

When you decide to use photographs in your visual design, thumbnail sketch the layout first.

Thumbnail Sketch

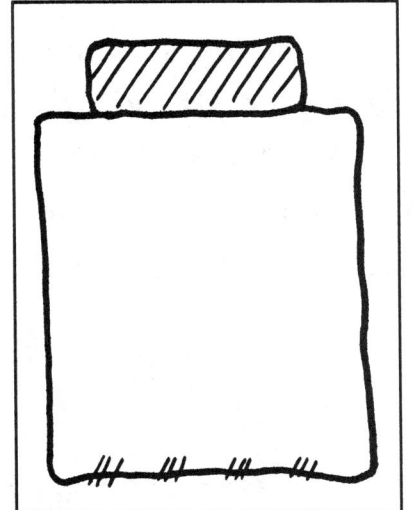  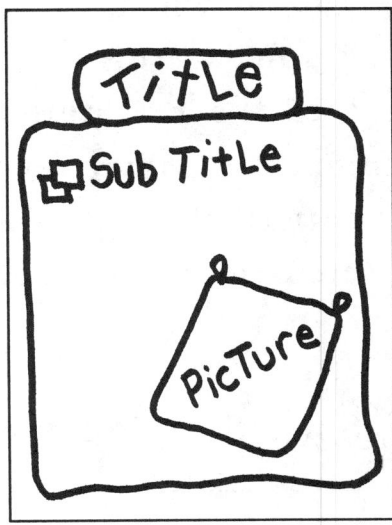

Layout: Portrait
Border Design
Title

Color Decision
Graphic Decision

Lettering Decision

Experiment with a variety of colors, borders and lettering styles that match your photograph.

After finalizing your design, transfer your ideas to paper charts, transparencies or computer screens

2. Pictographs

The second type of graphic image is a pictograph. A pictograph is a drawn image of a concrete item that looks much like the real thing. Pictographs are simple line drawings that are easily recognized, but do not have the detail of the actual object. You will find step-by-step instructions for creating pictographs in the *Graphics* section.

Some Sample Pictographs:

Person   Partners   Team

3. Ideagrams

An ideagram is the third type of graphic image. An idea-gram represents an idea or thought that is conceptual in nature. Use a combination of simple lines and symbols to illustrate difficult concepts or to show emotions. Step-by-step ideagram instructions can be found in the *Graphics* section.

Some Sample Ideagrams:

Idea   Rapport   Productivity

3. Iconotoons

The fourth type of graphic image is the iconotoon. This graphic represents an idea in a fun and humorous way. To create iconotoons, simplify the picture into icons and combine them with cartoon images.

Some Sample Iconotoons:

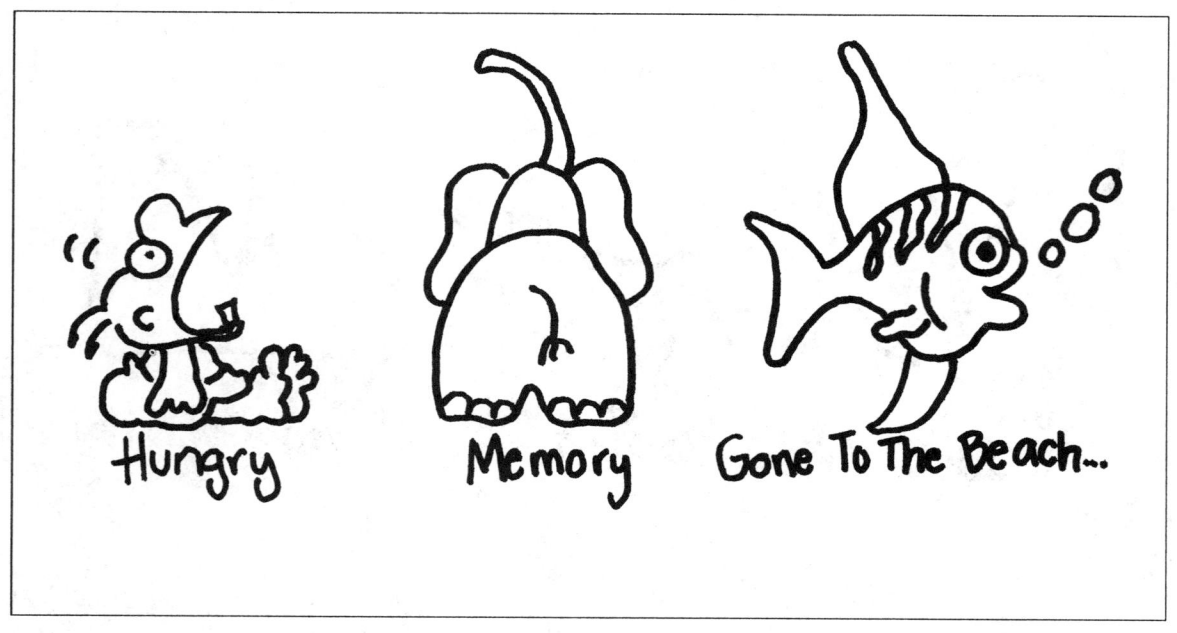

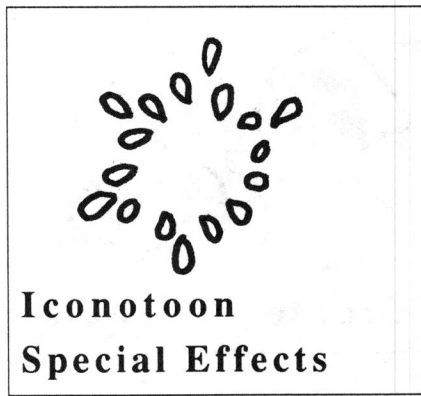

Iconotoon
Special Effects

Add special effect marks to show action, fun and emotions around iconotoons. You will find step-by-step drawing panels for creating iconotoons in the *Graphics* section.

Some Sample Iconotoon Special Effects Marks:

Starter Symbols

The last graphic image is a starter symbol. They separate, highlight and add interest to information. You can find creative starter symbols that appeal to you in graphic design books and magazines.

Some Sample Starter Symbols:

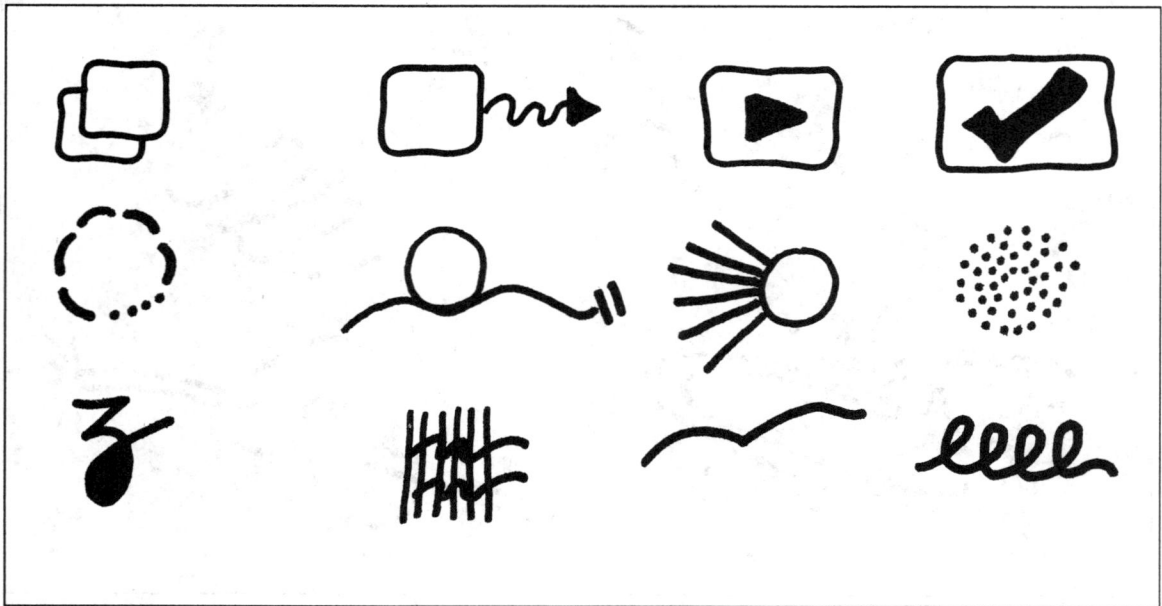

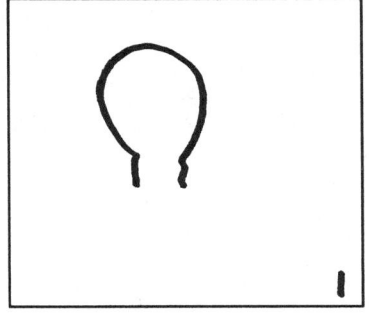  

Step-by-step drawing panels and practice drawing areas for Pictographs, Ideagrams and Iconotoons can be found in the *Graphics* section.

Examples of how to use the different graphic images in a visual are in the *Ready Made* section.

The Graphics

 **Creating Shapes**

 **Step-by-Step Panels**

 **Graphic Language**

 **The VIG Page**

The Graphics

Creating Shapes

EZ Guide s a y s: "If you can draw ⬭⬭⬭ "s, ▱ ▱ ▱ 's, △ △ △ 's and 〰 's --- you can turn words into pictures by creating terrific graphics!"

The Graphics - Creating Shapes

Whether your topic is detailed and complex or is difficult to visualize, your ability to communicate visually will greatly affect the amount of information your audience will understand and retain.

Simple hand drawn graphics can depict ideas, emotions and intangible concepts more easily and clearly than many spoken words.

Scientists and psychologists have found that the mind thinks in pictures --- at times the pictures are three dimensional holographs, multiplaned and in color! As a presenter, your job is to convey your content so the individuals attending will understand and remember your message. To accomplish this, your material must be presented in the way the mind thinks -- in pictures.

The easiest way to illustrate concepts, ideas, theories and complicated information is to draw a picture. This is nerve wracking, however, for those of us who feel we are artistically challenged -- to the point that we often state, "Oh, I can't even draw a straight line!" Well, the good news is, it doesn't take straight lines to create the graphics you are about to learn. It only takes the ability to combine four basic, every day shapes that you are already used to drawing!

Start by drawing the following four shapes:

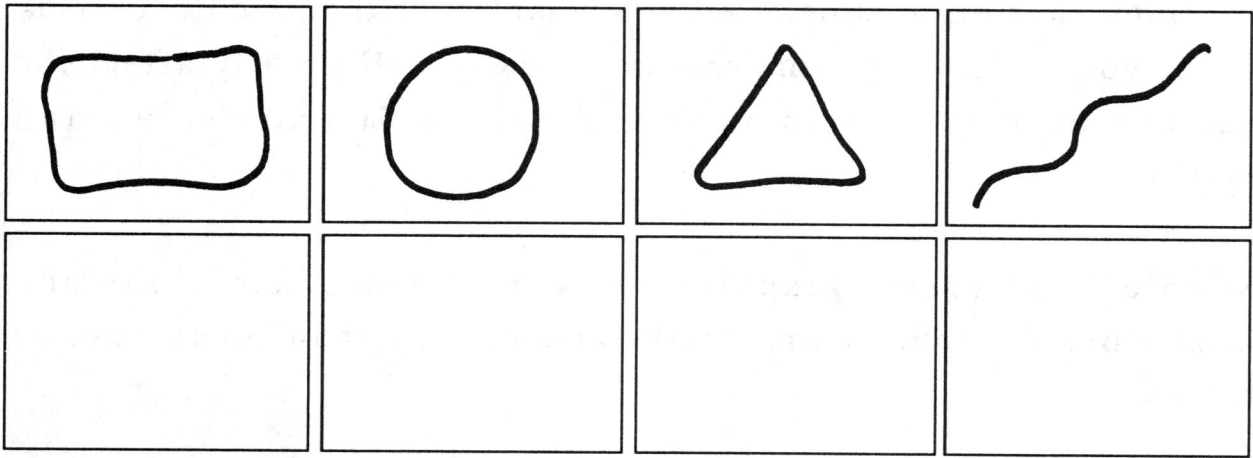

Then practice turning these shapes into graphics by copying the step-by-step panels as illustrated below:

RePort :

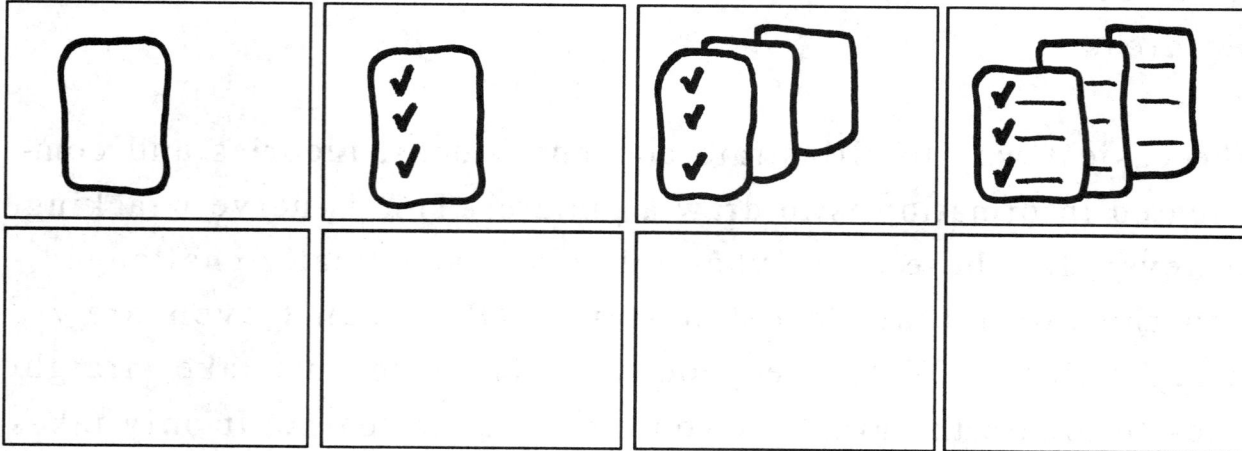

Planet

Trees

Direction

The Graphics

 **Step by Step Panels**

EZ Guide says: "If you look at children's art in kindergarten, you'll see great examples of graphic communication. Kids are able to draw with uninhibited glee! Amazingly enough, it is easy to recover your natural drawing ability just by practicing and combining the basic shapes you are about to learn with these step by step panels."

Turning Words Into Pictures --- Step by Step

The following drawing panels are provided as guidelines to help you practice combining shapes to create Pictographs, Ideagrams and Iconotoons (as described in the Images section of the *Basics Chapter*).

Copying is one way to learn how to draw. Notice how each graphic will begin with one of the basic foundation shapes and will continue to develop by adding additional shapes or lines to it.

Practice copying the shapes shown in each panel, then practice the various combinations on a sketch pad or in a sketchbook, until you can combine the shapes from memory.

Office Building

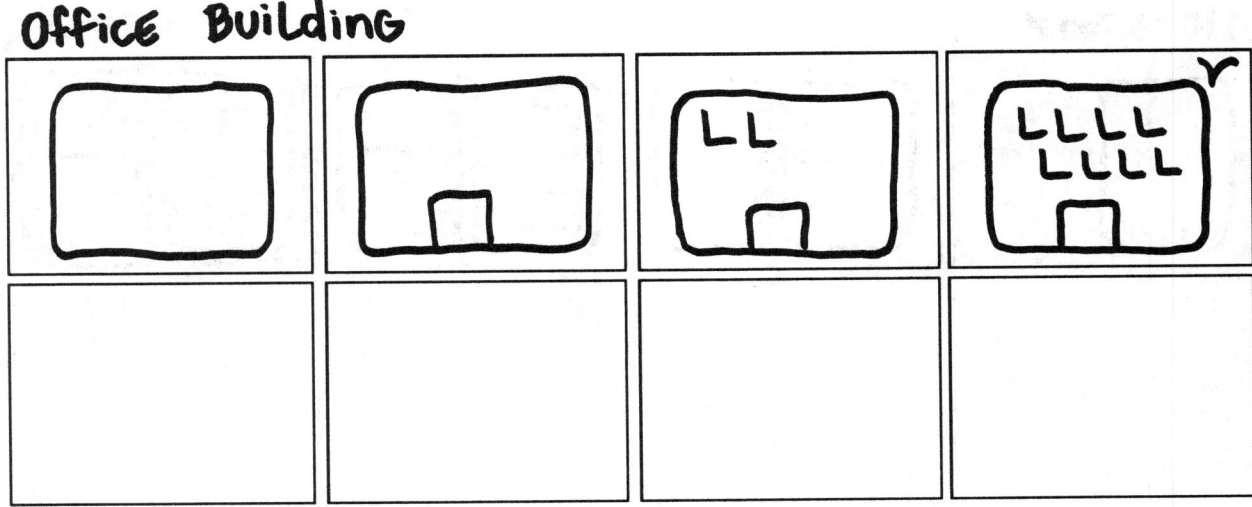

Pictograph Graphics --- Step by Step

To draw pictographs (as described in the Images section of the **Basics Chapter**), take an actual real life object and draw or copy it as close to the real thing as possible.

You will begin by focusing on the basic shape, adding some basic line strokes and then adding your own creative details to complete the pictograph.

Since repetition and practice are the best ways to increase your drawing capabilities, use your special drawing pen to copy the pictographs shown in the panels provided below them, repeating each step slowly and deliberately.

Notebook

Person

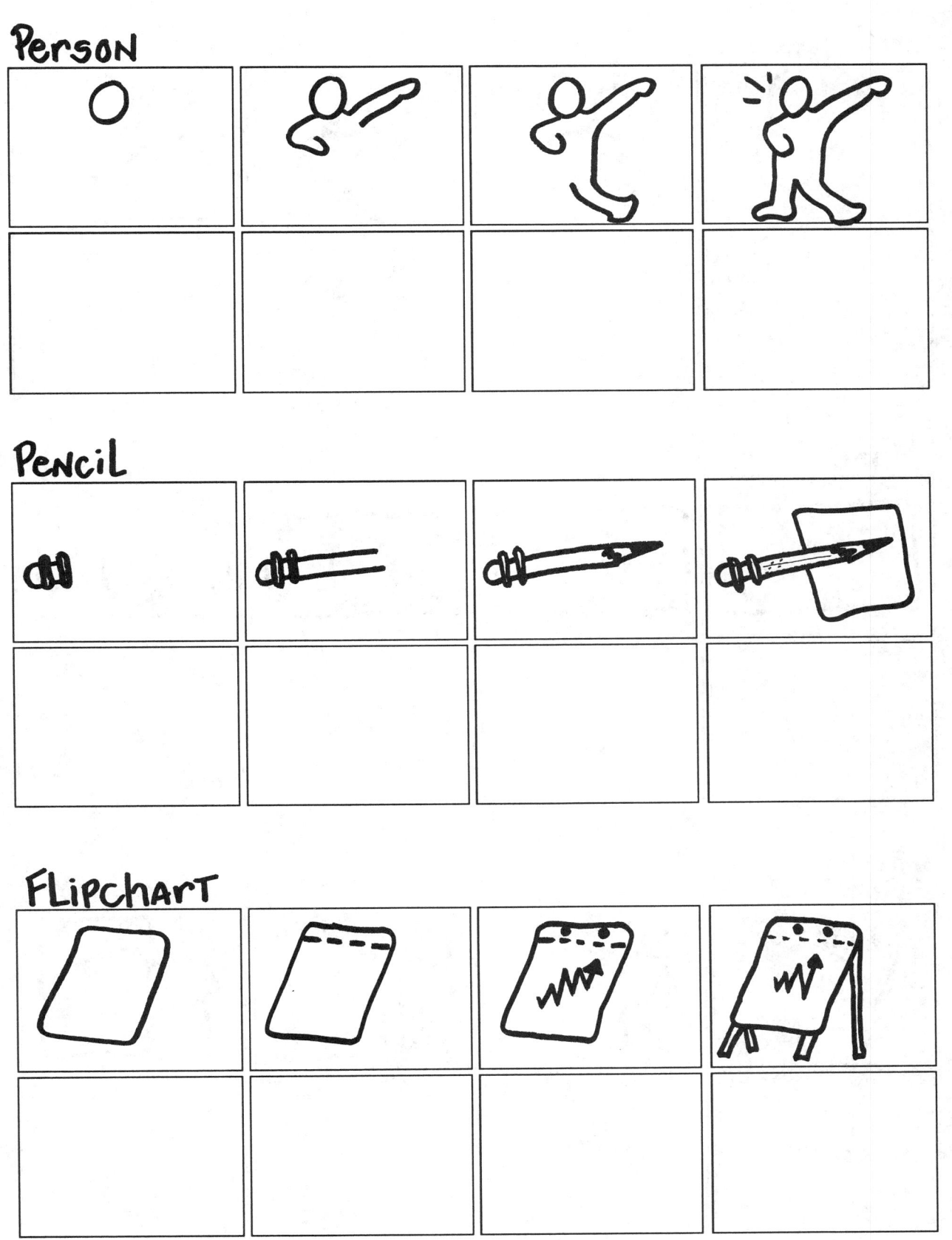

Pencil

Flipchart

Balloons

Money

Presenter

Ideagram Graphics --- Step by Step

Drawing an ideagram (as described in the Images section of the **Basics Chapter**), is slightly more challenging but by using the same basic shapes foundation, you can assign a graphic symbol or picture and create powerful images to illustrate your idea or concept.

Ideagrams are simple graphic images that represent an object. Usually, the graphic image is universal in nature and strongly associated with the image, almost like a word.

For example, for the word *love*, the ideagram is

Productivity

Conflict

Rapport

UPWARDLY MObiLE

MoViNG VeHiCLe

StoRM CLouds

Iconotoon Graphics --- Step by Step

Iconotoon graphics are the most challenging to draw but often prove to be the most useful because they truly turn words into pictures.

To create an iconotoon, (as described in the Images section of the *Basics Chapter*), combine cartoon effects with icons to illustrate objects in a humorous way.

Iconotoon face drawings are possibly the easiest and best way to illustrate emotions. Your main concern is to make sure your iconotoons are immediately understandable and that you will be able to draw them quickly and easily in front of your audience!

OucH !

Hungry

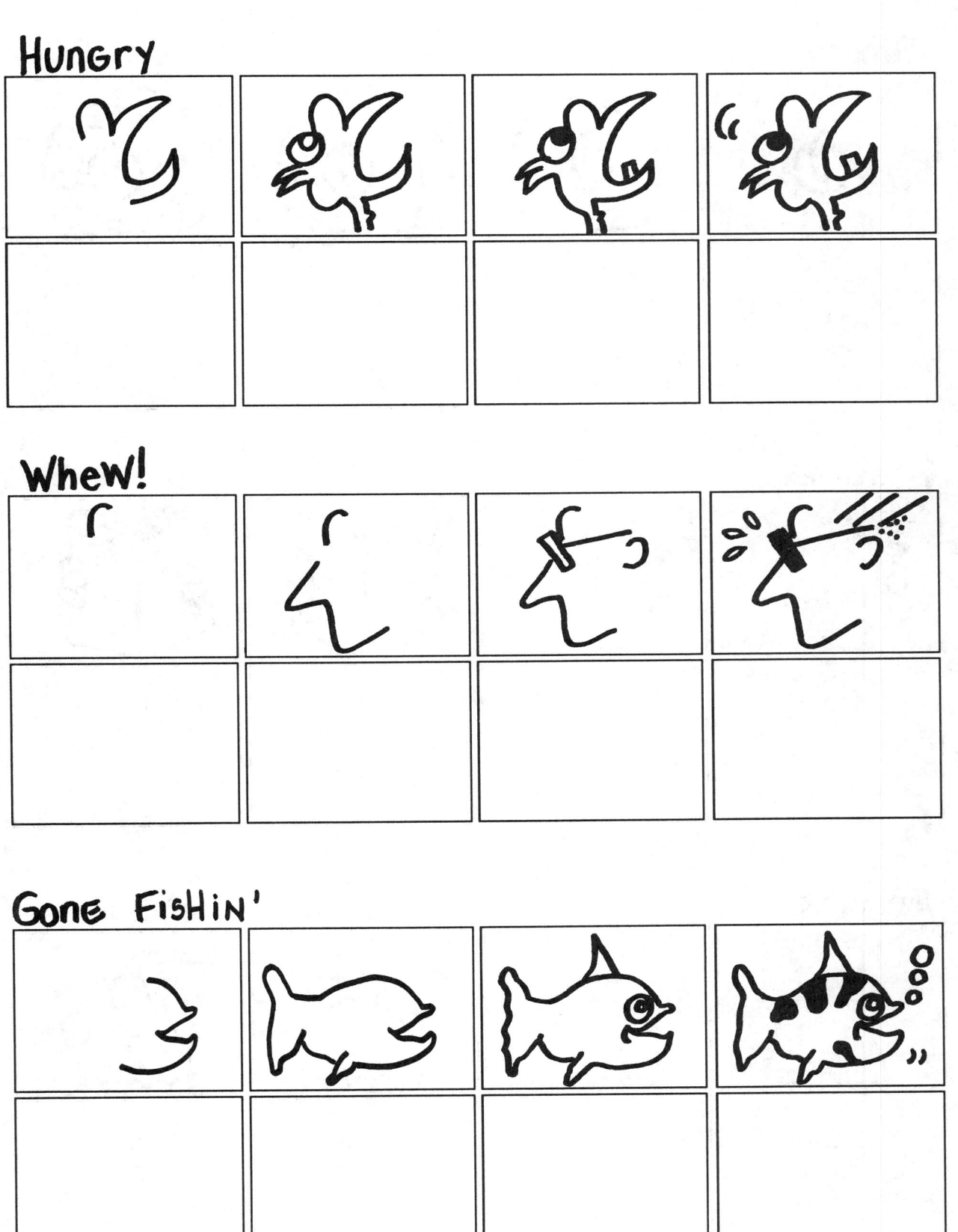

Whew!

Gone Fishin'

Timer

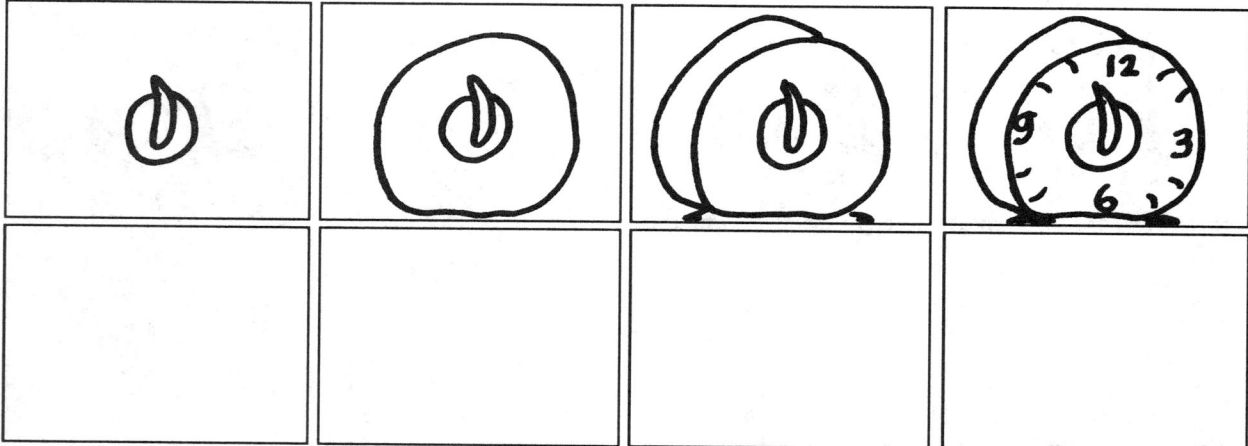

Reading

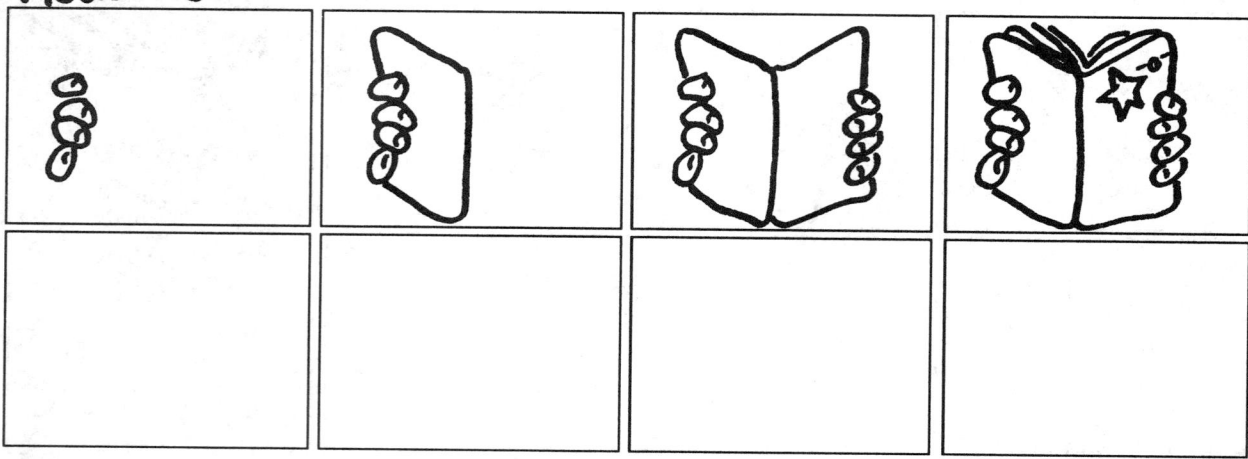

Memory

The Graphics

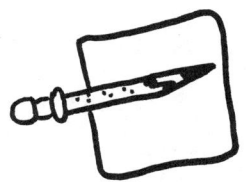 **Graphic Language**

EZ Guide says: "Because the mind thinks in pictures, your message will be so much more memorable if you can demonstrate your point by drawing those pictures quickly, easily and effortlessly!"

Creating Graphic Language

By using different combinations of lines, squares, circles, angles and cartooning effects, you can create your own graphic language library.

Many ideagrams and iconotoons (see **The Graphics Chapter**, *Step by Step section*) transfer easily into an instantly recognized graphic language. Your aim is to find easy and quick to draw pictures that relate directly to your concept or idea. We have provided some of our favorite graphic language symbols.

You'll find an area at the end of this section that you can use to practice our favorites and begin to create and add some of your own.

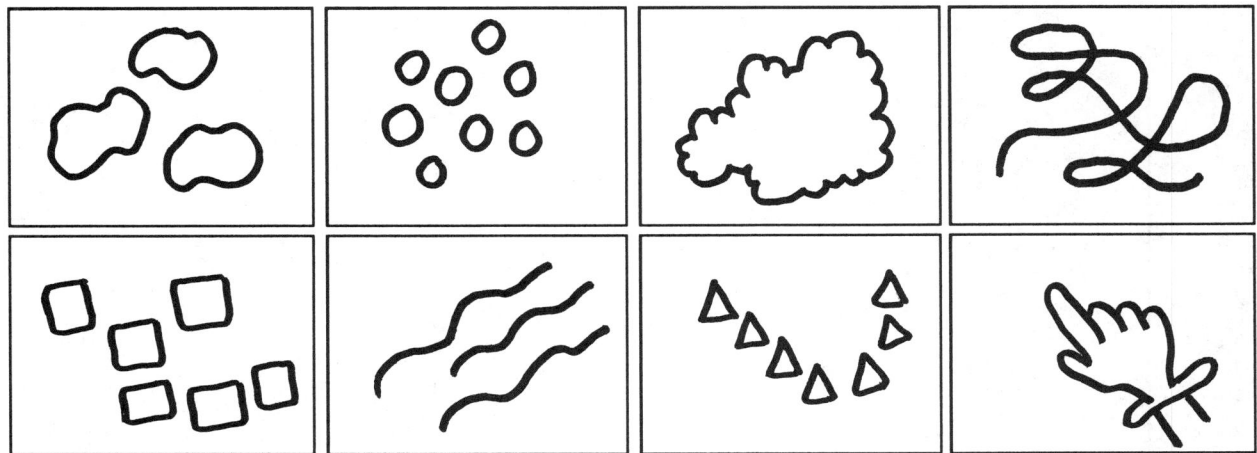

Action	Airmail	All That Jazz
Anatomy	Announcing	Artistic
Balance	Book Buddy	BZ As A Bee
Care	Charming	Continuous
Conversation	Comfort	Communication

COUNSEL

DIALOGUE

DIRECTION

FLYIN' HIGH

FRESH PAINT

FUN

GENERATE

GRAPH MAN

HELP!

HIGH FIVE

LEADERSHIP

LEAP

MAIL

MANAGEMENT

MEMORABLE

SIX TO GO

SYNERGY

TEAM

TEAM EFFORT

TEST THE WATERS

THANK YOU

THIS WAY

TIME TO GO

TO DO

TIME FLIES

TURN OVER A NEW LEAF

TRIP

VALUES

VISION

WEATHER

ASLEEP FRIGHTENED GLAD

HAPPY HUNGRY JOKING

LAUGHING NERVOUS ON VACATION

OUCH SAD SICK

SNOOZING TOUGH GUY WORRIED

The VIG Page

VIG = Very Important Graphic

EZ Guide says: "Use the **VIG** page tips about visual communication to inspire you to continue your efforts to reignite your natural design and drawing talents.

The VIG (Very Important Graphic) Page!

Include a WOW idea, like this **VIG** page, to renew and reignite the viewer's brain so it can absorb more information.

Do something unexpected in your visual. Include a surprise graphic, hide a clue, drop an unusual color. This **VIG** page is an example.

If your message and information is detailed or complex, you will want to refocus your audience every so often with an interesting or unusual graphic.

Test yourself by looking for basic shapes and lines in every graphic and picture you come across. Then, copy the graphic into your sketch book for future use.

Keep your visuals simple!

VIG tips you have discovered and plan to use!

The Quick & Easy Ideas

 **Visual Communication**

 **10 Minute Visual Ideas**

 **20 Minute Visual Ideas**

 **30+ Minute Visual Ideas**

The Quick & Easy Ideas

 Visual Communications

EZ Guide says: "Try to integrate as many different visual activities and approaches as you can!"

Visual Communication

Quick and Easy visual ideas are compiled from the ideas shared by corporate trainers, professional speakers and educators from the United States and Canada. We are ever so grateful to all of the individuals who have been so generous in sharing their creative thoughts.

Visual communication has the advantage of being understood faster and easier than the written word.

Since your audience can actually see ideas and solutions, they will absorb and retain visual information at an accelerated rate.

Visual Communication

Compare  to *"No Pedestrians Allowed"*

The visual difference emphasizes how easy it is to increase understanding and comprehension by using quick, easy to comprehend graphics. When people can apply these visual communication pictures to the presented information, the learning process becomes fun and successful.

Communicating visually is like athletics: if you don't practice, your creative abilities will get flabby and out of shape. You can avoid this breakdown in the creative approach to presenting visually by:

-Using versatility and simplicity as your creative guideline.
-Trying one new idea every time you create a new visual.
-Experimenting with new styles and graphics.
-Making visuals uncluttered, with facts displayed clearly.
-Creating large and easy to read titles and headings.
-Using up to three colors on your visuals.
-Making diagrams and pictures relevant to your message.
-Presenting your information briefly.
-Observing visuals everywhere to find new ideas.

The Quick & Easy Ideas

 ## 10 Minute Visual Ideas

EZ Guide says: "Here are some visual ideas and activities that only take 10, 20, or 30+ minutes to prepare!"

Visual Brainstorming

An easy way to brainstorm visually is to invite group members to write their ideas on Post-it Notes. Then, the group goes round robin, placing one Post-it Note on a flipchart or whiteboard at a time.

Cluster Post-its with similar ideas together. As the session continues, the Post-it Note ideas are movable, so that strategies and team planning can occur and ideas and action issues can be recorded and then assigned to different teams or group members.

Agenda Post-it Note Markers

Focusing everyone's attention on the day's agenda is easy with this Post-it Note idea.

Use a Post-it Note with a theme graphic as a place marker on the agenda. Or you can draw a graphic related to your content on a Post-it Note. As an example, if teaching a computer course, draw a mouse on it.

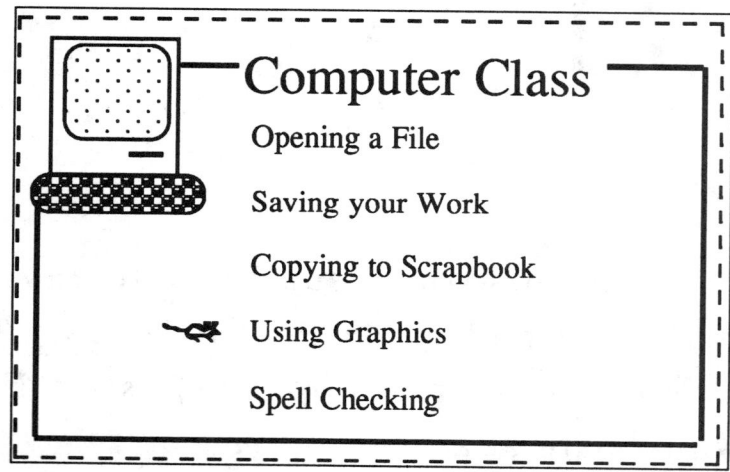

The agenda should be visible to the entire room. Explain that a Post -it Note place marker will mark the agenda items as information is covered. To assess what content is being taught, attendees can glance at the agenda displayed throughout the day. This also allows those who have drifted away from the lesson to quickly assess where the class is.

Creating Post-it Note Pointers

Cut a variety of pointer shapes and arrows from Post-it Notes. The shapes will stick wherever needed on any type of visual. They remain moveable, but not permanent.

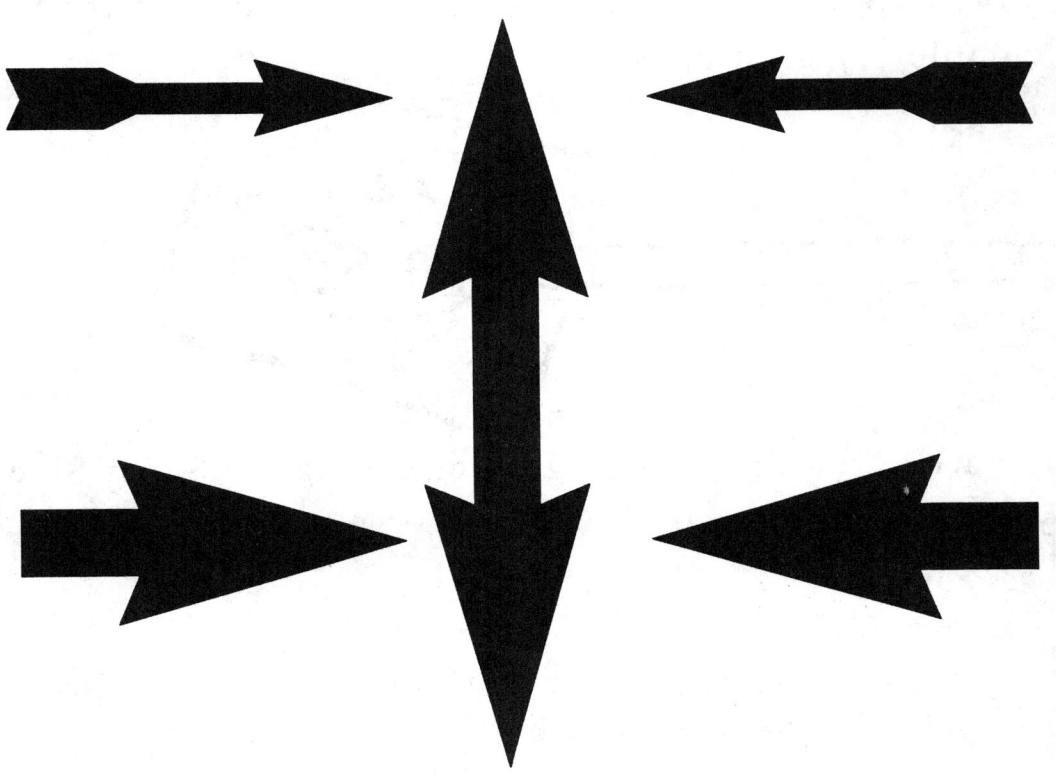

Super Sized Hand Pointer

A pointer designed specifically for use with flipcharts is now available. It is approximately eighteen inches long and contains a brightly colored crayon pointing hand at one end. The pointer can be used to underline or circle items on the chart by writing with the crayon finger or use it to simply point at key points on the charts. It comes in a variety of colors including red, blue, green, pink, orange and yellow. The crayon pointing hands are easily replaced once they are completely used up.

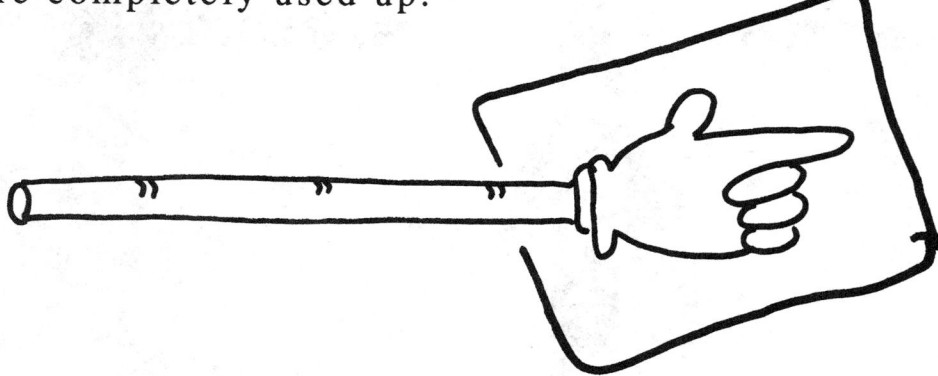

Call or write for a free catalogue containing the Super Sized Crayon Hand Pointer:

Tool Thyme for Trainers
4108 Grace King Place
Metairie, Louisiana 70002
Phone: (504)887-5558
Fax: (504)454-7911

<u>Tape Flag Identifiers</u>

The **3M** company makes Post-it Tape Flags in a variety of sizes and colors. To look more professional and prepared in your presentation, the flags can be used to reference, color code and easy access your visual charts.

The colored areas of the Tape Flags can be labeled with a permanent marker or ball point pen. Arrange the tape flags in a staggered fashion down the side of flipcharts to identify them as you create and draw them.

You can avoid stopping and searching for a chart that is already prepared .

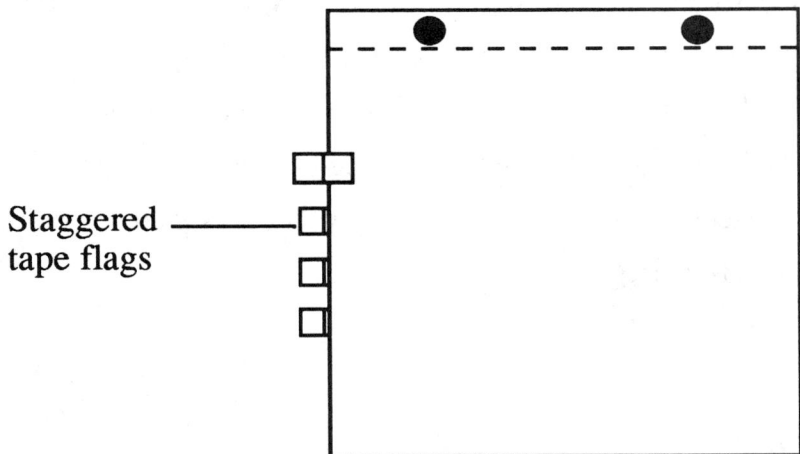

Staggered
tape flags

Electronic Visuals

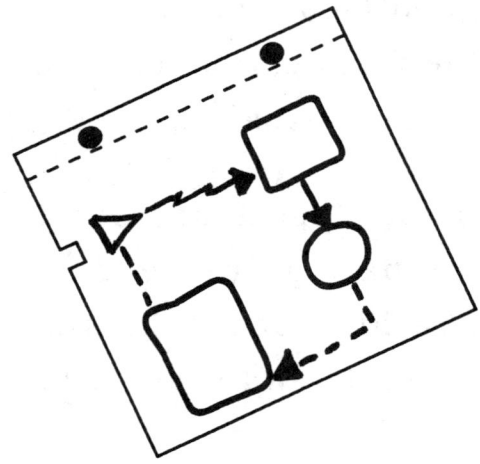

An electronic white board allows you to create visuals on a large white board and then provides your audience with instant copies of what you have drawn. A small copy-like machine located at the bottom of the easel provides the copies instantly. What a great time saver for distributing notes immediately rather than copying, typing and distributing them following the meeting.

The Quick & Easy Ideas

 ## 20 Minute Visual Ideas

EZ Guide says: "The more ways you are open to doing things, the easier it will be for you to communicate your message and ideas."

A Visual Parking Lot

During meetings or in educational settings, questions and issues can come up that the facilitator may want to put on hold until later. One way to deal with this is to use a visual known as a "Parking Lot."

Use a clean chart paper, draw a graphic that looks like a parking lot with spaces drawn for each "car". Place Post-it notes (regular or car-shaped) within reach of participants. If an issue or question comes up, ask the person who raised it to write it down on a Post-it and place it in a space on the visual parking lot. Before the session is over, deal with all the questions and issues on the chart inviting participants to join in answering the questions.

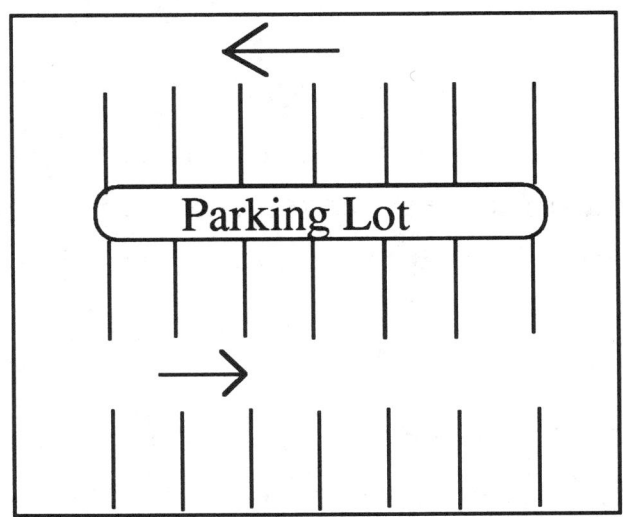

Visual Form Completion

When working and teaching the completion of new forms, this simple flipchart idea is terrific!

First, create a transparency of the form to be learned. Project the form on a clean easel chart so the entire form is visible. Use the image to demonstrate how to fill in the sample forms.

Then provide a fresh sheet for teams to practice on by turning the filled-in, used chart over the back of the easel.

Visual 3-D Objects

A simple and high impact visual idea is to use actual physical objects attached to your charts or white board or placed on top of your transparencies. Picking an object that is related to the content can make a dramatic attention getting point.

Sample 3-D Objects:

Idea	Represented By
Agenda Marker	Plastic hand
Attention to Detail	Eyeglasses, sunglasses
Break Time	Empty soft drink can
Infection Control	A surgical plastic glove

Select objects such as an actual machine part or a piece of equipment. This is quicker and easier than freehand drawing a picture of the item.

Chart papers still attached to the easel pad provide a more stable surface than single charts attached to the wall. For best results, use **Handi-Tak** (reusable adhesive) or **3 M** masking tape #232 or #234 when attaching the 3-D objects to the wall.

Cover Up Agenda Markers

Create a visual of your course agenda, placing checkmarks next to each agenda item. If the visual is a poster, cover the checkmarks with Post-it Notes. Use small physical objects. to cover the check marks on transparencies. As modules of the course are completed, remove the objects or Post-it Notes so the checkmarks become visible. Removing the cover ups allows the visual agenda to be used again and again.

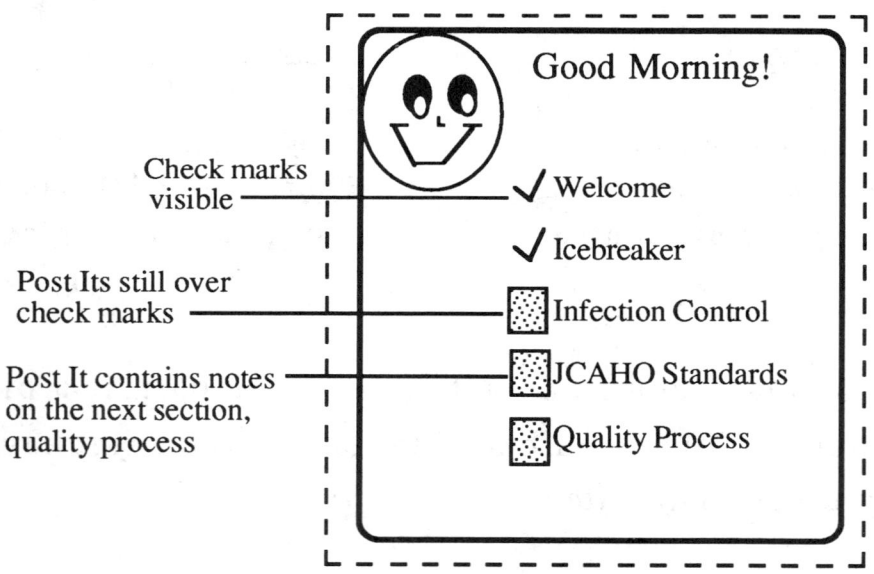

Cover up Post-it Notes can also serve as presentation notes by placing key content points on them. As the Post-its are removed, presentation of the next content item can be given without obvious notes.

Visual Dueling Activity

Place two easels at the front of the room.

Invite both a right and a left-handed scribe to record ideas learned in the session. This will allow each person to stand on a different side of the easel so that they can quickly record ideas and allows the group to see the charts as the ideas are recorded.

This activity encourages the quick free flow of ideas because, visually, it looks as if the scribes are racing each other to record the most ideas. It also frees the presenter to act as facilitator, encouraging and guiding the group's memory.

Visual Keyhole Cutouts

Visuals that use photographs, complex graphics or hand drawn pieces of artwork can be created quickly and easily by using a Quick & Easy 20 minute idea known as a keyhole cutout. A graphic is placed under clean, fresh piece of chart paper and a keyhole cutout opening is made with a razor like tool, (a coupon cutter or artists clip it), allowing the picture to show through.

How to Create a Keyhole:

On one of the last pages of a PaperChart pad, attach a picture or graphic. Use double stick tape or masking tape loops to attach the picture to the PaperChart so the tape will not show.

Pull one to seven pages down over the picture. Using a Clip It tool, cut out the paper laying directly on top of the picture, so that it shows through all of the pages.

If using lined or graphed chart paper, it will be easy to cut an even box out around the picture. If using plain, newsprint paper, draw curved lines with rounded edges around the image so a square box will not need to be cut without guidelines.

Cutting the keyhole through several sheets of clean paper allows for recording spontaneous audience input on the top page. When that page is full, flip it over and continue recording on the next page. The picture stays visible throughout the turning of the pages because the keyhole cutout allows it to be seen no matter which page is being written on. Continue to turn and record on a fresh page all the way down to the picture.

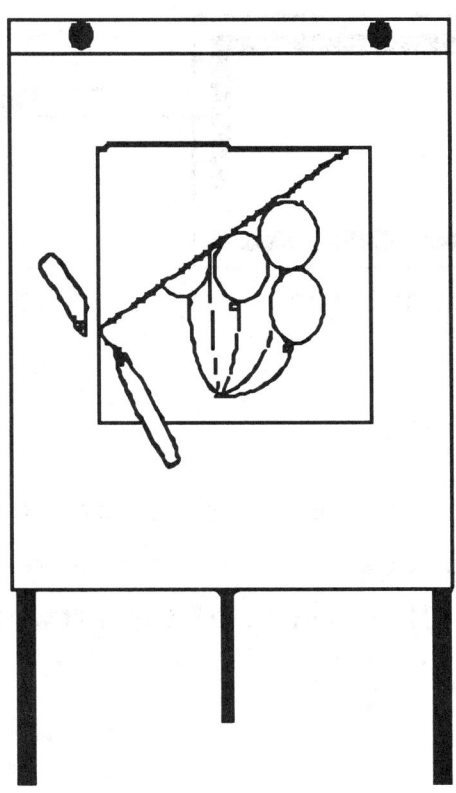

A quick and easy tip that will increase the life of the reusable keyhole artwork, graphic or photograph is to back them with a frame of thick, clear adhesive tape or **3M** masking tape. This will prevent destroying the artwork when removing it from the chart paper. New tape can be attached easily to the frame when ready to be used again.

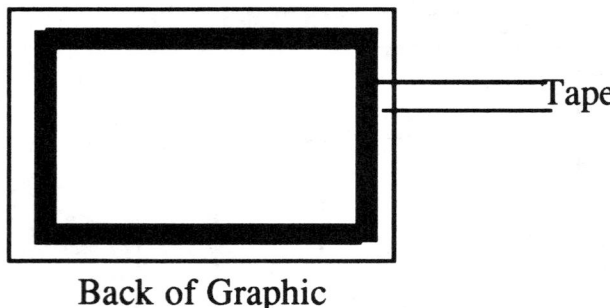

Tape

Back of Graphic

For the next session, reuse the same artwork, pull two to seven blank chart pages down over it and cut out a new keyhole. This will allow reuse of the artwork, picture or graphic indefinitely!

Practice keyhole cutout:

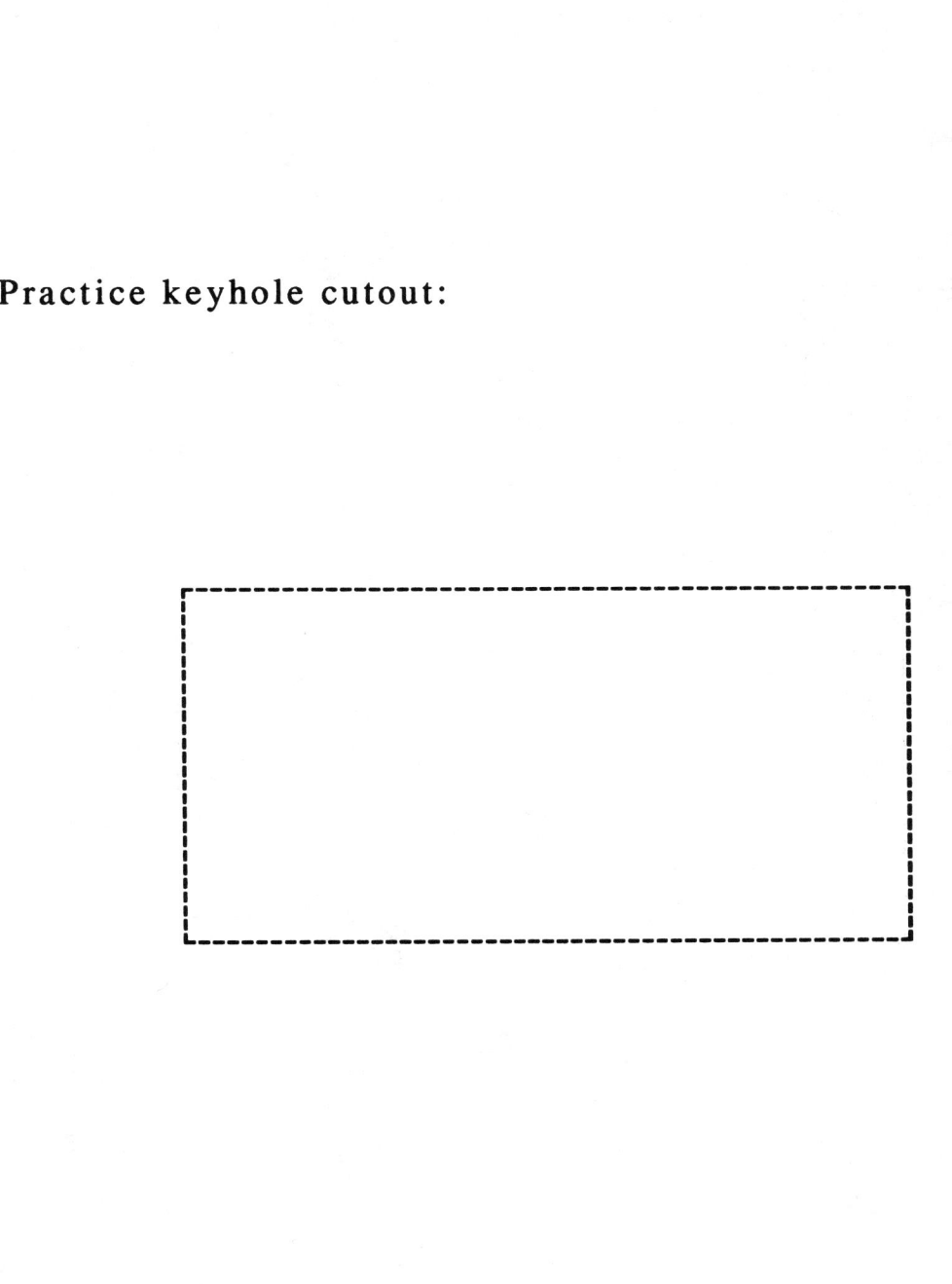

Practice cutting!

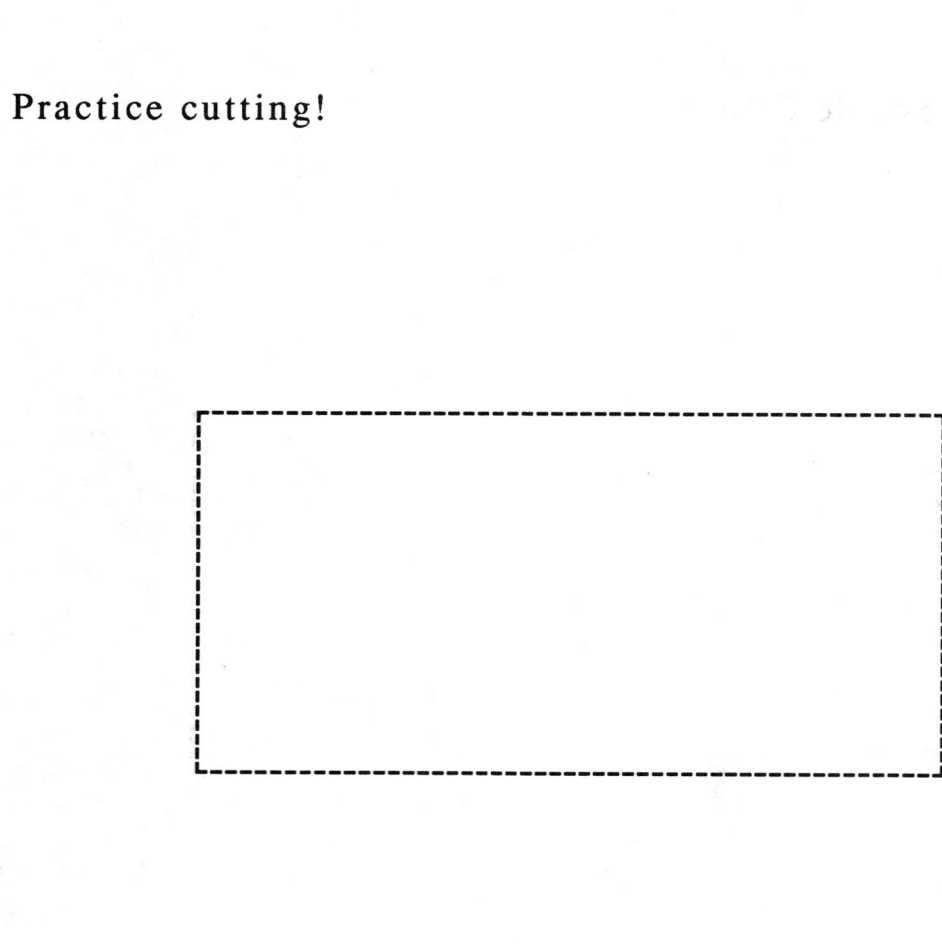

Visual Keyhole Cutouts

Use freehand artwork, photographs, clip art, computer graphics, content related items, anything that will visually portray your message.

The Quick & Easy Ideas

 **30+ Minute Visual Ideas**

·READING · RETENTION · NOTE ·
TAKING · READING · RETENTION ·
NOTETAKING ·
EZ GUIDE ·
·30 MINUTES·

EZ Guide says: "Allow your audience time for reading, retention and notetaking before removing your visuals."

Magic Paper Letters

This idea involves a series of visual paper letters that are used together in a presentation. Select a theme word directly related to the content message and make it into a point of interest in the design of the visual.

In the top left hand corner of the visual (or even in the border), place one paper letter per chart and present them in the order that will spell the selected word.

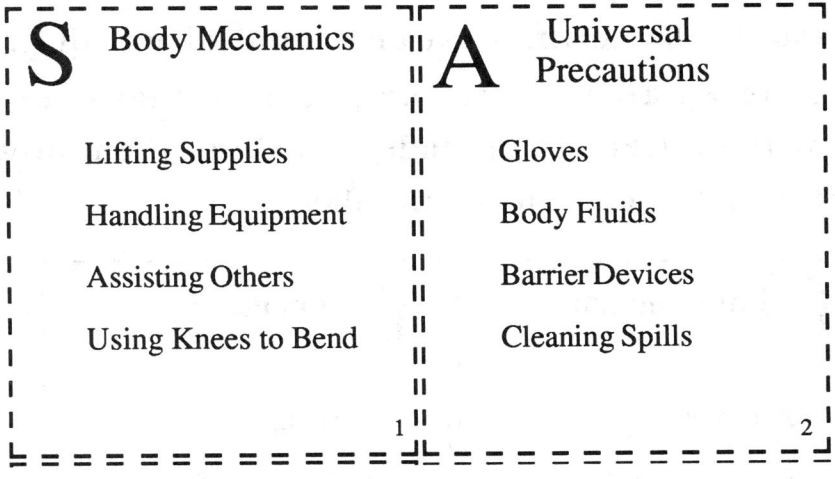

Continue to present the information without mentioning the letter placed in the corner. When someone notices the letters and deciphers the word, you can reward them!

Magic Paper Letters

F Fire Response

Rescue

Alarm

Confine

Extinguish

3

E Disaster Drills

Cardiopulmonary Arrest

Fire

Bomb Threat

Emergency Situations

4

At the end of your presentation, if the letters or word go unnoticed, ask participants if they can see anything unusual about the visual. Go to the first chart and direct their attention to the lettered area. Turn the pages so that everyone can see all of the letters. Conclude by asking them how this "word" relates to the content of the day.

T Environment

Accidents

Electrical Cords

Equipment

Spills

5

Y Personal

Parking

Off Campus Site

Psychiatric

6

S Body Mechanics

Lifting Supplies

Handling Equipment

Assisting Others

Using Knees to Bend

1

A Universal Precautions

Gloves

Body Fluids

Barrier Devices

Cleaning Spills

2

F Fire Response

Rescue

Alarm

Confine

Extinguish

3

E Disaster Drills

Cardiopulmonary Arrest

Fire

Bomb Threat

Emergency Situations

4

T Environment

Accidents

Electrical Cords

Equipment

Spills

5

Y Personal

Parking

Off Campus Site

Psychiatric

6

Visual Windowpanes

This visual communication technique organizes or "*chunks*" visual information into window-like boxes which serve as a memory cue. The technique taps into the spatial aspects of retention and is based on the concept that the short term memory can retain seven items at a time, plus or minus two. The maximum recommended number of window boxes is nine.

Advanced preparation time is needed, but visual windowpanes are easy to make and highly reusable.

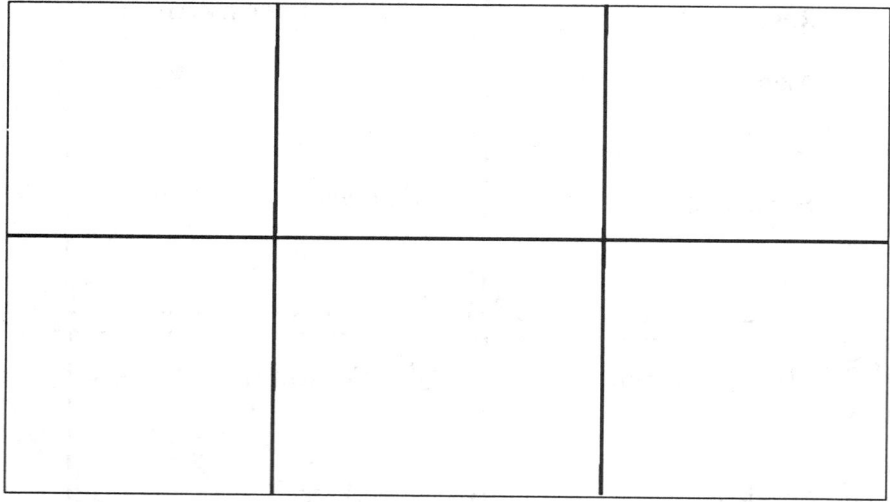

A concept is shown in visual format, one at a time, in each window pane box. As the concept is shown, an auditory explanation is given that ties the picture to the idea. Each box builds on the previous information shown, until all of the boxes are filled in. By involving your audience's visual and auditory senses, you have created a powerful memory tool.

A Windowpane Activity

An example of a windowpane used to teach the adult
Heimlich maneuver to lay persons according to American
Heart Association standards is shown below. The pictures in
each square key the memory to important points.

The presenter can place either a copy of computer generated graphics or freehand draw the figures in each of the
window boxes. Each step is followed by an explanation.

The audience is asked to record linear notes and draw a
copy of the windowpane boxes as each step is presented.
Periodically, to reinforce learning, ask the participants to
revisit the boxes they have drawn and restate the expla-
nations to themselves.

Adult Heimlich Maneuver Windowpane

There are nine steps taught in the order that the window-pane boxes are laid out. The boxes are read from top left to top right, continuing on to the middle row, from left to right and finishing with the bottom row, from left to right.

Step 1

In the top left corner, suspect person is choking, face is red, hands may be up around the throat, tongue is hanging out.

Step 2

The top middle box with the question mark represents the rescuer asking the choking victim, "Are you choking?"

Step 3

The top right hand box represents the universal symbol, SOS, with the rescuer saying to the victim, "I can help you!"

Step 4

The center row left box has a pair of arms coming together. This represents the rescuer standing behind the choking person, placing their arms around and under the victim's arms.

Adult Heimlich Maneuver Windowpane

Step 5
The center row middle box represents the rescuer making a special fist, placing the thumb inside of the fist.

Step 6
The center row right box represents the rescuer placing the special fist where **X** marks the spot, below the ribs and above the waist.

Step 7
The bottom row left box is a picture of a spinning top representing the rescuer placing their non-dominat hand on top of the already placed special fist.

Step 8
The bottom row center box is an upward pointing arrow representing the rescuer pulling up and back with both hands in order to dislodge the obstruction.

Adult Heimlich Maneuver Windowpane

Step 9

The bottom row right box represents success in dislodging the obstruction with a smiling face. The stick figure lying down represents waiting for paramedics if the victim has passed out or continuing the Heimlich maneuver until the person is no longer choking.

After the windowpane boxes have been taught and the sequence and pictures recorded, ask participants what each picture represents. They will remember most of the meanings, even if they were totally unfamiliar with the Heimlich maneuver.

To help cement retention of the nine steps and the pictures of the Heimlich Maneuver, switch to an empty windowpane and place your hand in any box. Ask learners what picture appeared in each of the boxes, and the meaning for each box. For maximum comprehension and retention, have the whole group shout out the answers as you move around the blank windowpane squares.

Windowpane Boxes

The purpose for creating visuals in this manner is to present a process that encourages high retention. Any other sequential process can be easily adapted to this format. Key concepts that are not sequential can also be adapted in this manner as long as the pictures used in the windowpane boxes are easy to recognize and remember.

A practice Windowpane:

Windowpane Boxes

A Master Copy

PosterPrinter Visuals

Visuals can be created by using a machine offered by Varitronics called the **PosterPrinter Plus.** This machine allows you to insert letter-size originals --text, graphics, or both -- and turns the original into a 23" x 30" poster sized chart. You can also switch the PosterPrinter to a double size setting and enlarge the same original to a 45" x 35" poster.

PosterLynx, IBM or Macintosh computer link-up capabilities, allows the printout of presentation graphs, posters, flip charts and banners. The special banner kit, included with the PosterPrinter, provides ready-to-use agendas, announcements, welcome graphics and letters/number originals.

Original photographs, schematics and flowcharts can also be used to create visuals with the PosterPrinter because of the machine's high resolution capabilities. Reverse imaging is available and a variety of different colored posters can be created using different colored printer paper rolls.

The Ready Made Visuals

 **Ready Made, Ready to Go**

5 Minute Quick Draw

 **10 Minute Fast Draw**

15+ Minutes Surprise Yourself!

The Ready Made Visuals

Ready Made, Ready to Go

EZ Guide says: "Oh, what a treat! You'll find time-saving and copy-ready graphic ideas next. Whether you have plenty of time to prepare your visuals in advance or just 5 minutes to sketch before you speak, use this section of the book to help you generate ideas."

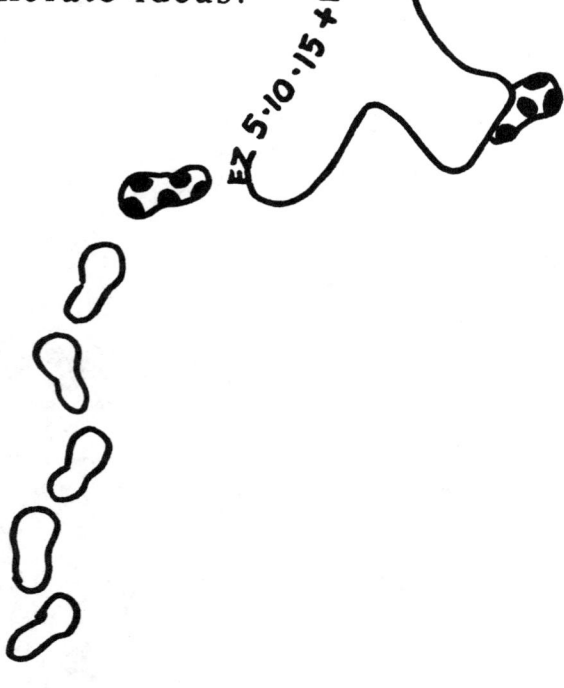

The Ready Made Visuals

Whether you are new or experienced at the art of creating visuals, use all of the following Ready Made examples to help you generate artistic ideas.

 Reproduce and use the Thumbnail pages to design and sketch visual layouts.

 Copy, enlarge and trace any of the borders, symbols or graphics. After tracing some of the graphics, rearrange and mix and match them to create new visuals.

 The sample visuals can be enlarged and reproduced into poster sized charts on a PosterPrinter Plus machine.

 Copy the Ready Made example onto a transparency and project it on an easel chart so the basic layout design and images can be traced onto flipchart paper.

 Once you have copied, traced or drawn your visual, laminate them for durability and indefinite use.

Thumbnail Sketches

The Ready Made Visuals

 5 Minute Quick Draw

EZ Guide says: "Here are some easy-to-copy visual ideas that only take 3 to 5 minutes to reproduce or draw!

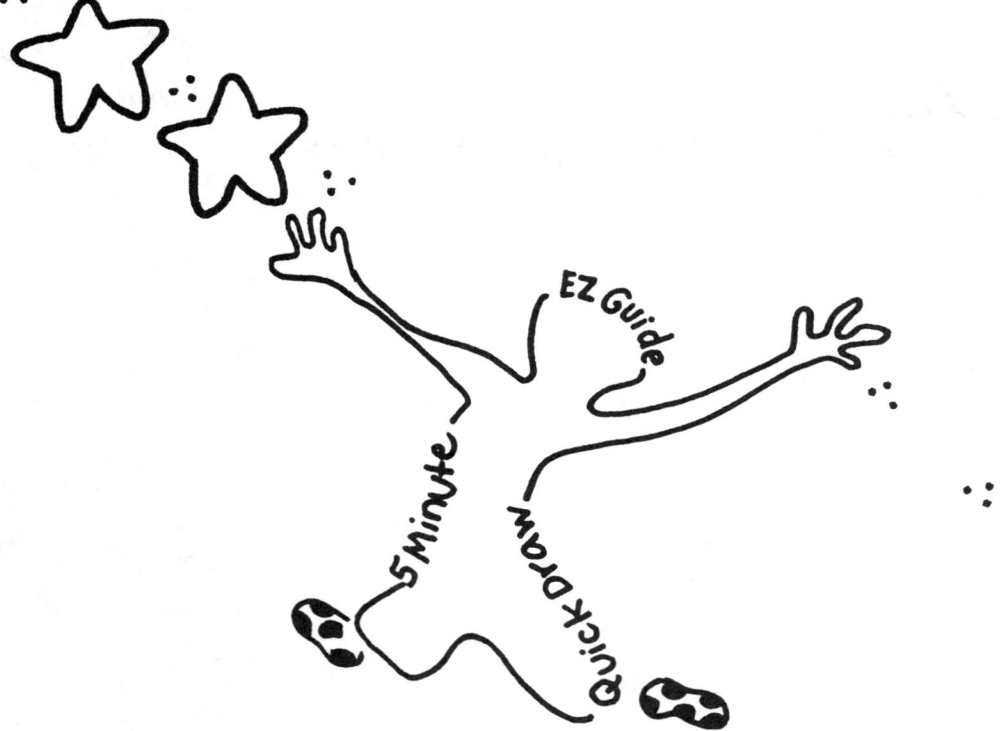

The Ready Made Visuals

 **10 Minute Fast Draw**

EZ Guide says: "Look at what you can create when you have 10 minutes!"

10 Minutes

EZ Guide

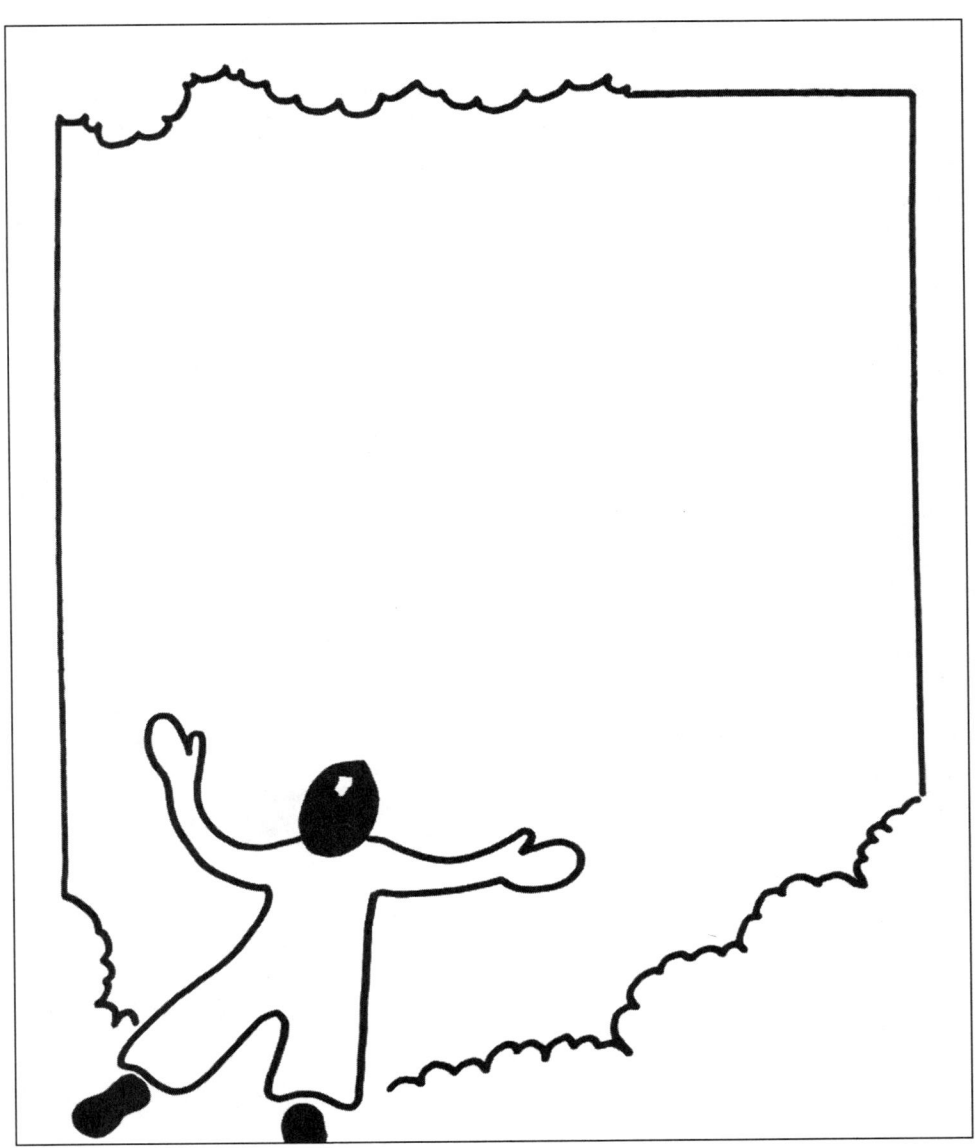

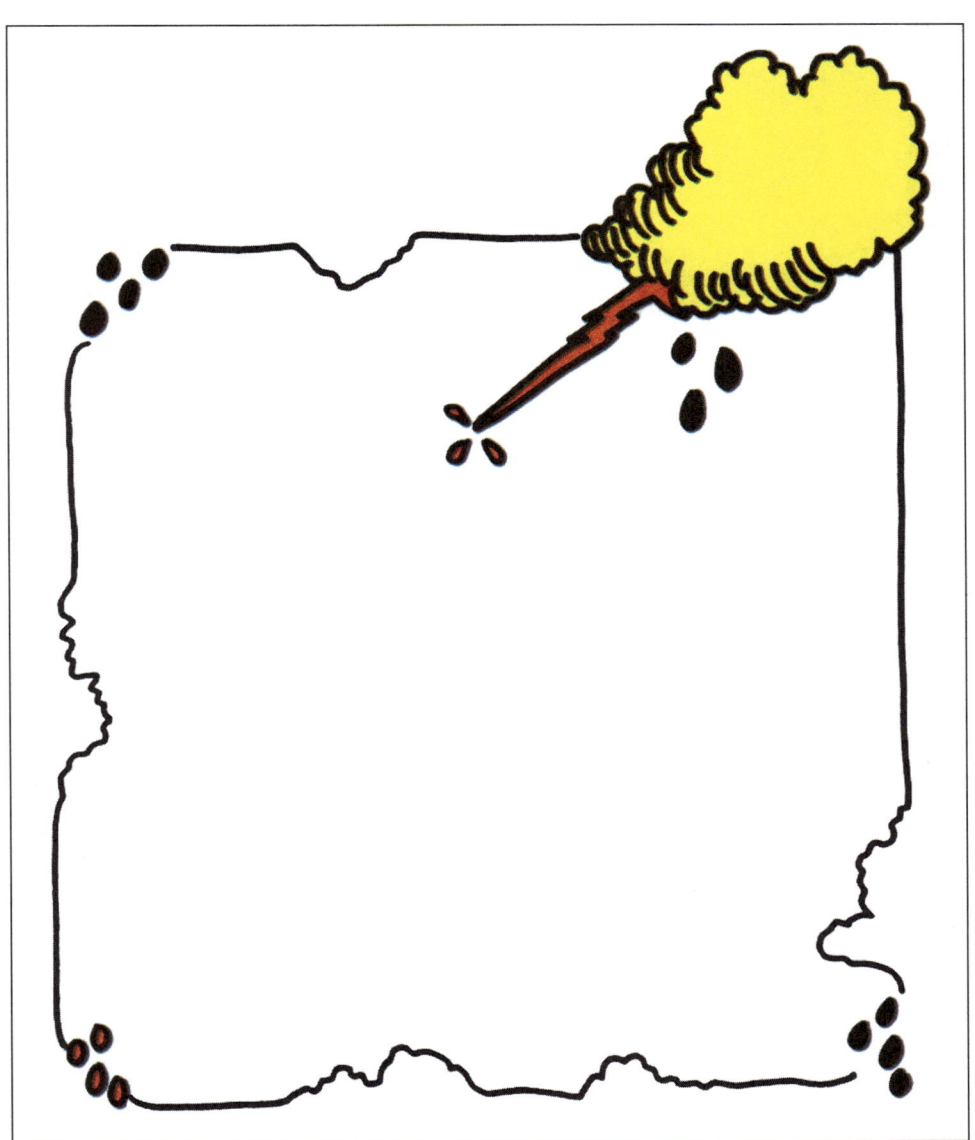

The Ready Made Visuals

 15+ Minutes Surprise Yourself!

EZ Guide says: "With 15 minutes or more, you can take your time, design, draw and color visual masterpieces!"

Final Thoughts

be free enjoy your moods
believe in yourself
celebrate your talent
draw every single chance you get
play eat cookies and ice cream
hug laugh make
friends with children
take couch time give drawing
supply gifts seek out
artistically challenged artists
and admire their
artwork

This book is designed to provide you with easy-to-draw graphics and visual ideas and examples that you can trace, copy or reproduce very quickly.

As you practice creating your visuals, try including:

- humorous graphics
  - different color combinations
    - outrageous cartoon characters
      - unexpected contrasts---
        tiny/huge
        light/dark
        smooth/jagged

Through our travels and research, we discovered that many presenters want to design and create visuals that vividly show what they are trying to say and that intrigue and fascinate their audiences. We hope our book will start you on a journey into visual thinking and communication.

Wishing you an abundance of imagination, ingenuity, courage -- and -- fun!

Lori Backer

Lori Backer

Michele Deck

Michele Deck

The Resources

EZ Guide says: Lori and Michele can custom design and create permanent visual sets tailored to your needs. For information on this service, phone or fax:

Tool Thyme for Trainers
4108 Grace King Place
Metairie, LA 70002
Phone: (504)887-5558
Fax: (504)454-7911

They are also available to conduct EZ Graphic Workshops either through Creative Training Techniques, Intl., (800)383-9210 or Tool Thyme for Trainers, (504)887-5558.

Backer, L., Deck, M., McCallum, D., <u>The Presenter's Survival Kit:</u> <u>It's A Jungle Out There</u>
   St Louis, MO; Mosby Yearbook 1995.

Backer, L., Pike, R. W., <u>Graphics and Visuals for Trainers</u>
   Edina, MN; Resources for Organizations, Inc., 1991.

Blitz, B., <u>How to Draw Blitz Cartoons</u>
   Philadelphia; Running Press, 1991.

Brandt, R., <u>Flip Charts</u>
   Richmond; Brandt Management Group, 1986.

Burgess, A., <u>The Do It Yourself Lettering Book</u>
   Watermill Press, 1991.

Cameron, J., <u>The Artist's Way: A Spiritual Path to Higher</u> <u>Creativity</u>
   New York, The Putnam Publishing Group, 1992.

Davis, C., Brown, C., <u>Comic Strip Fun</u>
   New York; Walter Foster Publishing, 1989.

Davis, C., Brown, C., <u>Felt Tip Fun</u>
   New York; Walter Foster Publishing, 1988.

Emberly, E., <u>Drawing Book of Faces</u>
   Boston; Little, Brown & Company, 1975.

Fleishman, M., _Freelance Illustrator or Designer_
    Cincinnati; North Light Books, 1990.

Glasbergen, R., _Drawing and Selling Cartoons_
    Cincinnati; North Light Books, 1993.

Hart, C., _Making Funny Faces_
    New York; Watson-Guptill Publications, 1992.

Liungman, C. G., _Dictionary of Symbols_
    Santa Barbara; ABC-CLIO, Inc., 1991.

Maddocks, P., _How To Draw Cartoons_
    New York; Guild Publishing, 1991.

Margulies, N., _Mapping Inner Space_
    Tucson; Zephyr Press, 1991.

Morris, N., _The Lettering Book_
    New York; Scholastic Inc, 1984.

Morris, N., _The Lettering Book Companion_
    New York; Scholastic, Inc., 1987.

SARK, A Creative Companion
    Berkeley; Celestial Arts, 1991.

Sibbet, D. A., A Workbook Guide to Group Graphics
    San Francisco; Sibbet & Assocs., 1981.

Striker, S., Kimmel, E., The Anti-Coloring Book
    New York; Henry Holt & Company, 1984.

Tatchell, J., How To Draw Cartoons & Caricatures
    London; Usborne House, 1987.

Tatchell, J., How To Draw Monsters, Animals & Machines
    London; Usborne House, 1988.

Tatchell, J., Varley, C., How To Draw Lettering
    London; Usborne House, 1991.

Viska, P., The Animation Book
    New York; Scholastic Inc., 1993.

White, J. V., Graphic Idea Notebook
    Rockport, MA.; Rockport Publishers, Inc., 1991.

Wilder, C., The Presentations Kit
    New York; John Wiley & Sons, Inc., 1994.

To receive your EZ Graphics Kit gift item, please remove and complete this original coupon.*

Name: _____

Address: _____

City, State, Zip: _____

Mail coupon to:

Tool Thyme for Trainers

4108 Grace King Place

Metairie, LA 70002

* Note: Only original coupons from the EZ Graphics Kit book will be accepted. Sorry, photocopied coupons can not be honored.